# 500
# pasta dishes

the only compendium of pasta dishes you'll ever need

Valentina Sforza

**SELLERS**
PUBLISHING

A Quintet Book

Published by Sellers Publishing, Inc.
161 John Roberts Road, South Portland, Maine 04106
Visit our Web site: www.sellerspublishing.com
E-mail: rsp@rsvp.com

ISBN: 978-1-4162-0909-6
e-ISBN: 978-1-4162-0960-7
Library of Congress Control Number: 2013931250
QTT.FHPA

This book was conceived, designed, and produced by
Quintet Publishing Limited
6 Blundell Street
London N7 9BH
United Kingdom

Photographer: Ian Garlick
Food Stylist: Valentina Sforza
Art Director: Michael Charles
Series Editor: Donna Gregory
Publisher: Mark Searle

10 9 8 7 6 5 4 3 2 1

Printed in China by 1010 Printing International Ltd.

# contents

# introduction

Although to most people pasta is as quintessentially Italian as the Sistine Chapel, many other cultures, particularly in Asia, enjoy their own kind of pasta in the form or stuffed dumplings or thin noodles. After all, there is a popular theory that the famous Venetian merchant and traveller — Marco Polo — brought pasta home from his journeys in China in the thirteenth century, and that his discovery was how spaghetti came into being! In Asia, noodles can be served in a soup, or stir-fried with meat, fish, or vegetables. Thai cuisine features a wide range of rice noodle dishes including many "pad thai" and various delicious salads and soups, and Vietnamese people are justly proud of their "pho," a dish consisting of broth, rice noodles, a few herbs, and meat. The word "pho" may be derived from the French "pot-au-feu."

Though the ties between pasta and Italian cuisine are undeniably strong, noodles really do come from all over the world. In the West, they are typically made from wheat flour, water, or egg. In Asian cuisine, noodles can be wheat-based, such as chow mien and udon, or made from buckwheat (soba), beans (cellophane), rice (rice vermicelli), or sweet potato (Korean vermicelli).

There is a further unmistakable similarity between wontons and other Chinese dumplings and the famous Italian filled pasta pockets like ravioli or tortelloni, especially when boiled or steamed and served in a soup, as opposed to being crisply fried. Gyoza wrappers, originally from China, but popular in Japan, are made with flour and water and are thinner than wontons, suitable for steaming but not sturdy enough for frying. Filled with a variety of delicious stuffings, such as minced pork, cabbage, chives, ginger, and garlic, they look very similar to ravioli and the principle is more or less the same, even though the flavors are very different.

Ukraine has a version of stuffed pasta, known as "varenikis," they are chewy and often served with a sweet dressing, but still unmistakably part of the pasta family.

In countries such as Austria, parts of Germany, Hungary, and Poland, noodles, or tagliatelle, are often served with rich dishes such as beef stroganoff, or beef or chicken paprikash, as an accompaniment to the main course rather than as a course in their own right, with a sauce or in a soup. In Germany and Austria, they have another version of pasta, made with flour and eggs. "Spaetzle" tends to be made with a softer dough, which is pressed through a ricer over boiling water, the result being a soft, dumpling-like pasta.

Mexican cuisine features vermicelli (thick spaghetti) in several recipes, although the interpretation could not be further from a classic such as a simple plate of spaghetti with a tomato sauce. For example, combining vermicelli with cilantro, shrimp, lime, and chiles makes for a delicious dish that is decidedly non-Italian.

Gnocchi are another food that loosely belongs to the pasta family. In Italy, they are made out of a variety of ingredients: spinach and ricotta cheese, spinach and stale bread soaked in milk, ricotta cheese, pumpkin, beetroot, potato, semolina, or potatoes, and are served with melted butter or a sauce. "Canederli" are bread dumplings that are only found in the northeast of Italy: Trentino-Alto Adige, Friuli, and part of the Veneto, where they are served as a first course or as a main course dish. Variations of canederli are common in all southeastern Europe, where they are also served as an accompaniment to meat stews and roasts. The word canederli, in fact, derives from the German and Austrian "knödel," which means dumpling.

Other Italian foods boast a fairly recent history, but their beloved pasta is much older, going back hundreds if not thousands of years. There is further proof that pasta was already being eaten in Italy even long before the voyages of Marco Polo, including clear archaeological evidence of an Etruscan type of pasta made from spelt flour called "laganum" (which is the origin of the modern word lasagne). However this food, first recorded in the first century CE, was not boiled and drained before dressing like pasta is now, or added to a soup, but was cooked in an oven.

Later, the Romans were the first to bake or fry their laganum, and the cut into strips in order to add them to other ingredients boiling in liquid, and so they created the first boiled pasta dish with other ingredients and a dressing to add flavor. It was called "laganum et ciceris," pasta with chickpeas, and some versions of this recipe are still very similar to the original ancient dish. In fact there is a version of the dish on page 76.

It is well known that the Arab invasions of the eighth century influenced the regional cuisine of Sicily and that of much of southern Italy. The most accepted theory for the introduction of pasta as we now know it is that it was born in Sicily under the name of "ittriya." It was a simple flour-and-water dough, twisted around a long stick to make something like a curly spaghetti. This product is most likely to be the original dried pasta. The modern word "maccheroni" derives from the Sicilian term for forcing the dough; early pasta making was a laborious and long-winded process. There are many Sicilian pasta recipes that still include other Middle Eastern ingredients such as raisins and spices such as cinnamon. This early pasta soon became a staple food in Sicily and subsequently spread to the mainland since durum wheat has always grown prolifically in Italy's climate.

By the fourteenth century, Italian dried pasta was very popular for its nutritional qualities and long shelf life, making it ideal sustenance for voyages at sea. Pasta made it around the globe during many voyages of discovery in the subsequent centuries. As new shapes and recipes evolved, pasta truly became a part of Italian life. The next and most significant development

in pasta came about in the nineteenth century, when pasta and tomato sauce were first combined. Despite having arrived in Europe shortly after their discovery in the New World, it took a very long time for the fruit to be considered edible. Until the mid-nineteenth century it was thought to be poisonous, an idea that might have had some foundation of truth as it is a member of the deadly nightshade or belladonna family. It was not until 1839 that the first pasta recipe with tomatoes was first documented. Shortly thereafter, tomatoes really took hold, especially in the south of Italy, and their use as a sauce for pasta became increasingly popular and has never waned.

Notwithstanding its popularity, pasta in Naples didn't get served at the tables of the aristocracy until after the fork was introduced towards the end of the eighteenth century, during the reign of King Ferdinand II. Until then it was considered to be strictly for the poor and was largely eaten as a street food, with the fingers. Once the use of the fork became widespread, pasta began to be served as a dish at banquets all over Italy and thereafter its spread around the world began.

President Thomas Jefferson (1743-1826) loved pasta and made it popular all over the United States. It seems that he first fell in love with a dish he sampled in Naples while he served as Ambassador to France. He promptly ordered crates of "maccheroni" and a pasta-making machine to be sent back to the States. Legend has it that the popular song Yankee Doodle Dandy, which contains the line "he stuck a feather in his cap and called it maccheroni" refers to this American episode in the history of pasta.

At the beginning of the twentieth century, the first, basic industrial pasta machines were installed in small factories on the coast near Naples, in towns such as Castellammare di Stabia. This area was chosen for its sea breeze which was considered perfect for the all-important drying process. Today modern technology allows the standardization of pasta production at every stage of the process, and factories can be found all over the country.

# fresh or dried?

There is a world of difference between fresh pasta and dried, durum wheat pasta; as well as all the sub-sections of dried egg pasta, whole-wheat pasta, dried soft-wheat pasta, and pasta made from other grains for consumers who suffer from a wheat intolerance but who still want to enjoy pasta as part of their diet.

## fresh pasta

Fresh pasta, the term usually used to refer to pasta made with eggs, is known in Italian as "pasta all'uovo" or "la sfoglia," and is mostly found in the northern regions of Italy. Because fresh pasta tends to be more delicate and sophisticated than dried durum wheat pasta, it does not suit all sauces. It is a pity to quash the delicacy of fine ribbons of freshly cut pasta such as tagliolini with a fiery sauce such as an arrabiata, which is much better suited to the substantial texture and flavor of a hard-wheat pasta such as spaghetti or penne. It is true to say that while almost any sauce can be used to dress hard-wheat pasta, only some should be used to enhance and flatter the special qualities of fresh pasta.

For many Italians, it is generally considered preferable to eat dried egg pasta (pasta all'uovo) that has been factory made and then dried, than soft fresh pasta made industrially rather than by hand. In Italy, especially in the northern regions, even the smallest town will have a small shop selling fresh pasta made by hand on the premises, which is the next best thing to making it oneself. But the idea of every Italian household making fresh pasta on a daily basis is something of a myth today, and there is no truth in the notion that fresh pasta is better than dried durum wheat pasta. They cannot be compared in this way, as they are so very different.

## dried pasta

Dried durum wheat pasta, in a classic shape such as spaghetti, requires a specific method of kneading, cutting, and drying. This means that it cannot be made at home in the same way that it is in a factory. Durum wheat pasta that has not been properly dried can fall apart when it is boiled. It is made with hard, wheat flour mixed with water, and in Italian is called "pasta di semola di grano duro." The gluten content of hard wheat is so high that is raises the overall protein content of this kind of pasta compared to types made with soft wheat flour which has a lower gluten content. This kind of pasta is eaten all over the country and each region has its own specific shapes. These are particularly good with the recipes that belong to those areas and many are part of a regional culinary tradition, so much so that some shapes may only be found in one region.

## whole-wheat pasta

Whole-wheat pasta has a strong flavor, which makes it difficult to appreciate the quality of the sauce used to dress the finished dish. Normal durum wheat pasta that is cooked al dente (firm to the bite) usually provides plenty of fiber. Conversely, if the pasta is overcooked it will turn into a solid, glutinous mass that is much harder to digest. It is important to respect the al dente rule because not only will the pasta dish taste so much better, it will also be much more beneficial from a digestive perspective.

## gluten-free pasta

Almost all sauces can be successfully used to dress gluten-free pasta, and there are countless brands, most of which are rather disappointing! With gluten-free pasta it always seems to me that the sauce becomes more important than the pasta as a carrier, because the pasta on its own is not always delicious. In my experience, one of the best brands of gluten-free pasta is made with brown rice and rice bran, and is called Tinkyada.

# which pasta with which sauce?

The best thing about pasta is that there are no hard and fast rules, but a few guidelines for matching your sauce to a particular pasta can be helpful.

Long pasta — such as tagliatelle, spaghetti and linguine — needs lots of lubrication, so they work best with olive-oil-based sauces which coat the pasta without drowning it.

Thicker strands, like fettuccine and tagliatelle, can stand up to cream sauces and ragùs (also known as bolognese).

Shaped pastas such as fusilli (twists) and conchiglie (shells) go well with all sort of sauces, but especially those with texture (lumps!). If you think about it those pieces of meat, vegetable, or bean are going to get caught up in the crevices and twists — which is a GOOD thing!

Short, tubular pastas like rigatoni and penne go well with sauces that are thick or chunky. Keep the size of the ingredients in mind: tiny macaroni won't hold a chickpea, while rigatoni may feel too large for a simple tomato sauce, where penne would work better. Ridged pastas provide even more texture for sauces to cling to.

# pasta tips

To achieve the best possible results for a plate of perfectly dressed pasta, known in Italian by the generic name of "pastasciutta," to distinguish it from baked pasta, stuffed pasta, pasta soups or salads, there are certain golden rules that must be observed:

- Pasta likes plenty of water to cook in when it is being boiled. The ratio is 5 1/2 pints of water for 1 pound of pasta.

- Make sure the water is properly salted before adding the pasta. The correct amount of salt is 1 1/2 teaspoons to 2 pints of water.

- Make sure the water is really boiling before you add the pasta to the pot.

- Replace the lid on the saucepan once the pasta has been completely immersed in the boiling water to return to the boil as fast as possible. Once the water boils again, remove the lid and continue the boiling process, stirring the pasta from time to time.

- The only way to really tell if pasta is cooked the way you like it is to fish a bit out of the saucepan and taste it. Once you are happy with the level of tenderness, drain the pasta and dress it quickly, bearing in mind that the pasta will continue to cook for as long as it is hot.

- Save some of the hot pasta water after draining the pasta to help distribute the sauce as you toss everything together; the addition of a little hot water at this point helps to prevent all the sauce being soaked up before the sauce has been evenly distributed. This is especially important when making pasta for large numbers of people.

- Remember that all fresh pasta cooks much more quickly, and that the al dente rule doesn't really apply when dealing with fresh pasta or pasta soups.

- Serve the pasta piping hot and never serve cheese with a fish pasta dish.

# about pasta machines

These are either hand-cranked, or the more complicated electrical versions. The hand-cranked model is favored by most, as long as it was made in Italy by an old-fashioned family firm such as Imperia or Augusta. These are good fun to use, almost impossible to break, and they give great results, making smooth — even silky — pasta. Nothing can beat a good rolling pin however, which easily stretches and flattens the sheet of dough, ready for cooking. To do the job properly, a pasta rolling pin needs to be extra long, and quite heavy.

### important tip for pasta machines

The most important thing to remember about these machines is NEVER to wash them, or allow any moisture to get inside the machine. It will never dry, and will definitely rust making it useless. After use, simply brush clean (you should only need to remove excess flour) and replace in the box until the next time you need to use it. Store in a dry place.

### extra attachments

It is possible to add attachments to the basic machine, such as a ravioli-making tray, but it is questionable whether these are as efficient as using a tabletop and a cutter or a sharp knife. Ravioli trays can also to bought separately.

### cutting shapes and electric machines

The basic machine cuts pasta either into tagliatelle or tagliolini/spaghetti, but other cutting units can be added on to make pappardelle or other long ribbon shapes. Electric pasta machines are usually able to make lots more shapes, including short ones such as penne or maccheroni. In the case of these machines, many of which make the dough as part of the operation, it is a question of following the instructions that will come with the machine.

# basic recipes

In this chapter, you will find the core recipes you will return to time and time again. It's worth practising them a few times, until you're really confident! Many of the dishes in this book are based on these basic recipes.

# la sfoglia — fresh pasta

see variations page 29

Fresh egg pasta is relatively easy to make at home, especially with a hand-cranked pasta machine to help make the sheets of pasta as fine and evenly rolled as they need to be. Learning how to achieve the same smooth, silky, paper-fine effect by hand, with a rolling pin and plenty of elbow grease, is considerably more difficult and requires several attempts. The basic dough is made from a blend of flour — either soft wheat flour, or a combination of hard wheat flour and soft wheat flour — with eggs. When making fresh egg pasta from scratch, quantities are measured in eggs.

per person:
1 extra-large egg
1 cup (4 1/2 oz.) plain white pasta flour or 50:50
    blend of white flour and fine semolina

Put all the flour in a pile on a work surface and plunge your fist into the center to make a hollow. Break the eggs into a bowl and use a fork to beat together until well combined. Pour the eggs into the hollow, and begin to mix the eggs into the flour with the fork. Once more or less combined, use your hands to pull everything together and start kneading.

This is not like making pastry, so this is not the moment for a delicate approach, but if you are too heavy handed you will cause the dough to dry out too much and it will never roll out smoothly! Knead the flour and eggs together until you have a very smooth, pliable ball of dough that feels cool to the touch and springs instantly back when gently pressed with a fingertip. Cover with a clean cloth or wrap in plastic wrap and rest in a cool place for at least 20 minutes, this will relax the gluten and make the dough more manageable.

*continued on page 20*

When the dough has rested, roll it out as thinly as possible with a strong, long, heavy rolling pin. Form it back into a ball, and roll it again. Repeat until the dough is really elastic, smooth, and shiny. It should cool down considerably as you work it, and you will feel it dropping in temperature as you go along. When it is ready the sheet of dough will feel like a brand new, wrung out, damp chamois leather, but must not be brittle. Keep it moist by covering it with a slightly damp clean cloth when you are not working with it.

If you use a pasta machine instead of the traditional rolling pin, knead together the eggs and flour to create a ball of dough as above. Rest the dough, wrapped, for at least 20 minutes, then break off a piece about the size of a small fist and cover the remainder to prevent it drying out. Flatten this section with your hands and push it through the widest setting on your pasta machine. Fold this in half and repeat. Do this twice or more, until you hear the pasta snap as the rollers force the air pocket to burst. Move the machine down to the next setting. Repeat twice. Continue in this way, changing the setting after every second time, until you're using the last or penultimate setting on the machine, depending on how fine you want the pasta to be. Lay the sheet of pasta carefully on to a floured surface to dry until papery, when you can then cut it into the desired shape, or use immediately while still moist if you wish to make ravioli, tortellini, or any other filled pasta. Repeat until you have worked all of the dough. Keep an eye on the sheets of pasta you have already rolled out; they will not be easy to cut if they are too dry. To keep them moist, cover with clean, slightly damp cloths.

Cut your pasta into the desired shape as soon as it is dry enough to roll up without it sticking to itself. Once cut, you can use the pasta immediately, or let it dry out further. If you are making a filled pasta shape such as ravioli you must use soft, moist pasta otherwise it will be impossible to close each one securely. In this case, fill the pasta at once, and then leave the shapes to dry.

Freeze fresh pasta on trays, then place in bags and label. Use frozen pasta within one month.

# basic tomato sauce with garlic

see variations page 30

This is the most fundamental of all the tomato sauces; it is essential to make all kinds of garlic-based sauces taste right and is the sauce from which classic sauces such as puttanesca and arrabiata are born.

3 to 5 tbsp. richly flavored extra-virgin olive oil
2 to 4 cloves garlic, crushed and left whole

1 (14-oz.) can whole tomatoes, roughly chopped
Salt and freshly ground black pepper

Fry the garlic very gently with the olive oil in a heavy-bottomed saucepan or skillet. Don't let the garlic color or it will give a bitter flavor to the sauce. If the garlic goes brown, or even black, discard both it and the oil, wipe out the pan and start again. When the garlic is soft and pungent, remove the garlic from the pan and discard. Pour in the tomatoes and stir carefully. Simmer over a lively heat for about 10 minutes or until the sauce is glossy and thick. Season to taste and cover. Take off the heat and keep warm until required for dressing your pasta.

*Makes enough sauce for 6 portions of cooked pasta*

# tomato sauce with soffritto

see variations page 31

This is another primary tomato sauce, this time with a softer background flavor thanks to the onion, carrot, and celery fried together gently at the start of the cooking process. Learning how to make this properly will mean that sauces like a classic bolognese will end up tasting so much better. If you have them, a few celery leaves, added with the other vegetables, make a good addition.

1 medium-sized onion
1 large stick celery
1 large carrot

4 tbsp. extra-virgin olive oil
1 lb. whole canned tomatoes
Salt and freshly ground black pepper

Peel and chop the onion very finely. Scrape and wash the carrot, then chop finely. Wash the celery, tear away the strings, and then chop finely. Pour the oil into a heavy-bottomed saucepan and add all the chopped vegetables. Fry together very gently and slowly until the vegetables are soft and the onion becomes transparent. Only at this point, add the tomatoes and stir thoroughly. Cover and leave to simmer for about 30 minutes, stirring regularly. Season to taste and use as required.

*Makes enough sauce for 6 portions of cooked pasta*

# fat-free tomato sauce

see variations page 32

This is a really light sauce, perfect for slimmers and summer suppers. Make sure you let it reduce once you have sieved it, as it can be too watery if you don't. It is only worth making this sauce with fresh tomatoes when they are in season; at other times of the year, used good quality canned tomatoes instead.

1 1/2 lbs. fresh, very ripe tomatoes
1 large stick celery, quartered
1 large carrot, quartered
1 large onion, peeled and quartered

7 or 8 sprigs of fresh basil
7 or 8 sprigs fresh flat-leaf parsley including stalks
Salt and freshly ground black pepper

Place all the vegetables and the herbs in a saucepan. Cover and place over a low heat. Allow to simmer slowly until pulpy. Then cool and push through a food mill or sieve (alternatively blend in a food processor, and then push it through a sieve.) The result will be a fairly liquid sauce (more like soup) which you will need to reduce until thickened. To do this, pour the sauce into a saucepan over a medium heat and let it boil quickly without burning. Keep an eye on the sauce and take it off the heat when it is the consistency you want. Add salt and pepper to taste.

*Makes enough sauce for 6 portions of cooked pasta*

# béchamel sauce

see variations page 33

Béchamel sauce is also known as white sauce, and is made with a roux of butter and flour, to which milk is added. It is one of the four mother sauces of French cuisine and is used in many Italian recipes, including lasagne. It is also used as the base for many other sauces, including mornay, soubise, and sauce crème.

1/3 cup (2/3 stick) unsalted butter
4 level tbsp. all-purpose flour
1 1/2 pints milk

Salt
Pinch grated nutmeg

Melt the butter over a low heat in a saucepan. When the butter is foaming, but before it begins to color, add the flour and mix together until a yellow paste is formed and is coming away from the sides of the pan. Pour in all the milk and whisk vigorously to prevent any lumps forming and to ensure everything is perfectly blended. Add the nutmeg and salt to taste and simmer gently for about 15 minutes, stirring constantly with a wooden spoon.

When the sauce is thick enough to coat the back of a spoon, and you can no longer taste the flour, take it off the heat and cover the surface with a little cold water to prevent a skin from forming, or cover it with plastic wrap. Set aside until required, then remove the plastic wrap and stir before using. If the sauce has thickened too much with cooling, return to the heat, and warm through, stirring, before using.

*Makes enough sauce for 4 servings of lasagna*

variations

# fresh pasta

see base recipe page 19

### spinach pasta
To make green pasta, omit one egg and replace with about 2 cups of pureed spinach, squeezed as dry as possible and added to the beaten eggs. Then proceed as main recipe

### squid ink pasta
Use about 1 teaspoon of squid ink to every 4 eggs, or more if you want the pasta to be even darker.

### extra-rich pasta
To make really rich, eggy pasta, use only egg yolks and, as the result will be quite dry, add a little water, very gradually, to help turn the dough into a glossy, springy ball.

### herby pasta
Add a small handful of chopped fresh herbs such as flat-leaf parsley, basil, or sage to the beaten eggs and blend into to the flour to create dough that is speckled with herbs when rolled out.

variations

# basic tomato sauce with garlic

see base recipe page 22

### basic tomato sauce with caramelized garlic
Fry the garlic until pungent and just beginning to brown around the edges, then discard and pour the tomatoes into the garlic-flavored oil and proceed as main recipe.

### basic tomato sauce with extra garlic
To make a stronger, more garlicky sauce, peel and puree the garlic, then fry it very gently in the oil for about 2 minutes before adding the tomatoes.

### smooth tomato sauce with garlic
To make a sauce with a smoother texture, use passata instead of canned tomatoes.

### basic tomato sauce with herbs
To add more flavor and color to the sauce, mix in some finely chopped basil or flat-leaf parsley, or both, to the sauce, at the very end of the cooking time.

variations

# tomato sauce with soffrito

see base recipe page 25

### sweet tomato sauce with soffrito
To make this sauce taste even sweeter and richer, add a glass of red wine to the vegetables and boil off the alcohol before adding the tomatoes.

### tomato sauce with soffrito & pesto
To give the sauce a summer kick, add a tablespoonful of good quality pesto to the sauce just before using.

### smooth tomato sauce with soffrito
For a really smooth sauce, use passata instead of canned whole tomatoes.

### smoky tomato sauce with soffrito
For a smoky flavor, add 1/4 teaspoon of smoked paprika to the chopped vegetables once they are soft, then continue as normal.

### creamy tomato sauce with soffrito
For a creamy sauce, add two or three tablespoons of fresh heavy cream or cream cheese just before using.

variations

# fat-free tomato sauce

see base recipe page 26

### rich tomato sauce
Stir in 2 tablespoons unsalted butter or olive oil at the end, when the sauce
is still hot, until melted and the sauce is glossy and shiny for a richer (but
not fat-free!) sauce.

### fat-free sauce with basil
Add a handful of ripped fresh basil leaves at the end, just before tossing
with pasta.

### fat-free spicy tomato sauce
For a spicy note, stir 1/4 teaspoon cayenne pepper into the sauce at the end.

### tomato sauce with pesto
To make the sauce take on another dimension, stir 1 tablespoon of good-
quality pesto into the sauce at the end of cooking.

### pasta salad with fat-free tomato sauce
Use this sauce cold, to dress freshly cooked, cooled pasta, to make a salad.
Add finely chopped scallions and 1/2 peeled, cubed cucumber, and mix
together thoroughly.

variations

# béchamel sauce

see base recipe page 28

### simple macaroni cheese

Preheat the oven to 350°F. Prepare the basic béchamel sauce, and add 2 cups grated Cheddar cheese at the end. Cook 2 2/3 cups macaroni until al dente, then drain and transfer to a 9-inch square baking dish. Mix the béchamel sauce with the pasta, and top with 1 cup grated Parmesan cheese. Bake for 20 minutes, or until golden. Let stand for 5 minutes before serving.

### cheat's lasagna

Preheat the oven to 350°F. Prepare a bolognese sauce (pages 47 and 116), and the basic béchamel sauce. Blanch 9 dried lasagna sheets until al dente. Cover the bottom of a 9-inch square baking dish with 1/3 of the béchamel sauce. Lay blanched lasagna sheets to cover without overlapping, then add 1/2 of the bolognese sauce. Repeat, ending with a layer of béchamel sauce. Top with 1 cup grated Parmesan cheese, and bake for 30–40 minutes. Let stand for 5 minutes before serving.

### cheesy vegetable, bacon & pasta bake

Preheat the oven to 350°F. Prepare the basic béchamel sauce, adding 2 cups grated Cheddar cheese at the end. Parboil 3 cups fresh vegetables (such as broccoli, green beans, carrots), drain, and toss in the béchamel sauce. Transfer to a 9-inch square baking dish, and top with 1 cup grated Parmesan cheese. Bake for 20–30 minutes. Let stand for 5 minutes before serving.

# classic italian pasta dishes

Here are my own tried and tested versions of all the much-loved dishes, with a few alterations to the authentic, traditional versions. Feel free to make your own variations to these classic dishes, or follow one of my suggestions.

# traditional christmas tortellini

see variations page 58

This wonderful soup is traditionally made by hand and served to the family at Christmas.

3 tbsp. unsalted butter
4 oz. pork loin, cubed
2 oz. turkey breast, cubed
4 oz. thick-cut mortadella, cubed
4 oz. thick-cut prosciutto crudo, cubed
2 eggs, beaten
5 tbsp. freshly grated Parmesan cheese
Large pinch grated nutmeg
2 x quantities fresh pasta (page 19), rolled into
   thin sheets and covered with a damp cloth

1 large chicken
3 carrots, topped and tailed
3 onions, peeled and halved
2 sticks celery
2 tomatoes, halved
2 cabbage leaves
7 pints cold water
Salt
Handful of fresh flat-leaf parsley, chopped

Make the tortellini: Melt the butter and fry the pork and turkey for 10 minutes. Process in a food processor with the mortadella and prosciotto. Stir in the eggs, Parmesan cheese, and nutmeg. Roll the pasta very thinly, cut into 3-inch squares, and place a little filling in the center of each. Fold over, to make a triangle shape. Push the base of the triangle in to make a small dent, and then bring the edges of the triangle together, and seal.

Make the broth: Place the chicken in a large saucepan with the vegetables, the cold water, and a little salt. Bring to the boil slowly and leave to simmer gently for about 2 hours. Leave to cool in the pot. Once cold, lift out the chicken and put to one side. Strain the liquid through a fine sieve. Leave to stand, remove any fat that forms on the top, and strain again. Bring this broth to a gentle boil and add the tortellini. Simmer until the tortellini are cooked (2–3 minutes), take off the heat, stir in the parsley, and transfer to a soup tureen to serve.
*Serves 6*

# pasta carbonara

see variations page 59

Traditionally served with bucatini (hollow, fat spaghetti), this is the traditional and original recipe for a classic carbonara.

14 oz. bucatini or spaghetti
Salt
3 oz. pancetta, guanciale, or best quality streaky
   bacon, cubed

4 eggs, beaten
6 tbsp. grated pecorino cheese
Plenty of freshly ground black pepper

Bring a large saucepan of salted water to the boil. Put the pasta into the water and stir thoroughly. Replace the lid and return to the boil. Remove or adjust the lid once the water is boiling again. Cook according to the packet instructions until al dente.

While the pasta is cooking, fry the pancetta in a very hot skillet until crisp and the fat has run. Meanwhile, beat the eggs in a bowl with the cheese and plenty of black pepper. When the pasta is cooked, drain and return to the pot. Pour over the eggs and cheese and the pancetta immediately and stir everything together, so that the eggs lightly scramble and pull the dish together. The fat from the pancetta should sizzle and fry as it mingles with the pasta. Serve at once.

*Serves 4*

# spaghettini with garlic & olive oil

see variations page 60

Lots of versions of this classic Roman recipe exist, but this is my time-honored version, eaten thousands of times, in all sorts of situations, but especially late at night.... This is the ultimate after-party food!

14 oz. spaghettini
12 tbsp. extra-virgin olive oil
3 cloves garlic, peeled and lightly crushed

Salt and freshly ground black pepper
2 tbsp. fresh flat-leaf parsley, chopped

Bring a large saucepan of salted water to the boil. Put the pasta into the water and stir thoroughly. Replace the lid and return to the boil. Remove or adjust the lid once the water is boiling again. Cook according to the packet instructions until al dente.

While the pasta is boiling, heat the oil and garlic together until the garlic goes completely black. Discard the garlic and keep the oil hot. Timing is quite crucial, as you don't want the oil to burn, yet it must be hot.

Drain the pasta and return to the pot, pour over the hot oil and seasoning, and mix together thoroughly. Mix in the parsley. Serve immediately.

*Serves 4*

# pasta with bacon, tomato & chile

see variations page 61

Amatrice, where this dish comes from, is a small town near Rome which is famous for its fantastic pork products. This is a real classic, rich and piquant, flavored with deliciously smoky pancetta. One of the few traditional sauces which uses garlic and onion.

8 oz. smoked pancetta, cubed
4 tbsp. rich extra-virgin olive oil
1 onion, peeled and finely chopped
3 cloves garlic, peeled and chopped
1/2 to 2 dried red chile peppers (according to preference), seeded and chopped finely

1 1/2 (14-oz.) cans whole tomatoes, drained and coarsely chopped
Salt
14 oz. bucatini or other dried pasta with a chunky shape
3 oz. pecorino or Parmesan cheese, grated

Fry the cubed pancetta with the oil until the fat is transparent and running freely. Add the onion, garlic, and chile to the pan and fry together gently until the onion is soft and translucent. Add the tomatoes and simmer covered for 20 minutes, stirring frequently, until the sauce is thick and glossy.

Bring a large saucepan of salted water to the boil. Put the pasta into the water and stir thoroughly. Replace the lid and return to the boil. Remove or adjust the lid once the water is boiling again. Cook according to the packet instructions until al dente.

Drain the pasta thoroughly and return to the pot, then pour in the sauce and mix together thoroughly. Serve immediately, with the cheese offered separately.

*Serves 4*

# penne arrabiata

see variations page 62

Cheese is not normally served with this recipe, which is called "penne al'arrabiata" in Italian. However if you or your guests insist on having cheese it has to be aged, peppery pecorino.

4 cloves garlic, peeled and finely chopped
1 to 4 dried red chiles, whole
4 tbsp. extra-virgin olive oil
2 1/2 cups canned tomatoes, chopped

Salt
2 2/3 cups (14 oz.) penne
1 tsp. fresh flat-leaf parsley, chopped

Fry the garlic and chile in the olive oil until they are slightly blackened. Discard the chile and add the tomatoes to the pan. Season with salt and simmer for about 20 minutes.

Bring a large saucepan of salted water to the boil. Put the pasta into the water and stir thoroughly. Replace the lid and return to the boil. Remove or adjust the lid once the water is boiling again. Cook according to the packet instructions until al dente.

Drain the pasta, and return to the pot. Pour over the sauce and mix together. Transfer to a warmed serving dish and sprinkle with the parsley before serving.

*Serves 4*

# la puttanesca

see variations page 63

This is a real classic and the flavors need to be really well balanced so you can taste them all. It is traditionally served over freshly cooked spaghetti, tossed together with a little extra olive oil and chopped parsley.

3 cloves garlic, peeled and lightly crushed
8 tbsp. extra-virgin olive oil
8 anchovy fillets (either salted or canned in oil, rinsed and dried)
1 to 4 small dried red chile peppers, chopped finely
1 heaped tbsp. salted capers, rinsed, dried, and chopped

1 1/4 cup best-quality passata
Generous pinch dried oregano
Salt and freshly ground black pepper
1/2 cup dry white wine
Handful stoned black olives, roughly chopped
2 2/3 cups (14 oz.) penne or spaghetti
Handful fresh flat-leaf parsley, chopped

Fry the garlic and half the oil together with the anchovy fillets and the dried chile peppers, until the anchovy dissolves. Remove the garlic, add the capers and the passata, and stir together thoroughly. Simmer for a few minutes, and then add the oregano, seasoning, wine, and olives. Stir and leave to simmer gently for at least 15 minutes (cooking it for longer will do no harm).

Bring a large saucepan of salted water to the boil. Put the pasta into the water and stir thoroughly. Replace the lid and return to the boil. Remove or adjust the lid once the water is boiling again. Cook according to the packet instructions until al dente. Drain the pasta, and return to the pot. Pour over the sauce and mix well. Serve immediately, with a little extra olive oil and the parsley.

*Serves 4*

# bolognese ragu

see variations page 64

This classic pasta sauce is usually used to dress tagliatelle rather than spaghetti. Keep the meat relatively chunky, so that the end result looks like a delicate stew.

4 oz. pork loin, boned
4 oz. beef steak, boned
4 oz. prosciutto crudo
1/3 cup unsalted butter
1 carrot, finely chopped
1 stick celery, finely chopped
1 onion, finely chopped
2 oz. pancetta or bacon, finely chopped

1 heaped tbsp. tomato puree diluted with
    8 fl oz. hot water
salt and freshly ground black pepper
1 1/2 cups hot broth or water or red wine
4 oz. chicken livers, washed and trimmed
6 tbsp. heavy cream
14 oz. mafaldini pasta (or tagliatelle)

Chop the meats together finely with a heavy knife. Melt half the butter and fry together the vegetables and pancetta or bacon for 5 to 6 minutes, stirring. Add the chopped meats and stir together to sesal all over. Add the diluted tomato puree, and season to taste. Stir thoroughly, cover and leave to simmer very slowly for about 2 hours. During this time never let it dry out, but stir frequently and keep adding a little hot water, broth, or red wine. After about 4 hours, when all the meat is tender, finely chop the chicken livers and add to the pan. Simmer for just 5 minutes. Then stir in all the cream and remove from the heat.

Bring a large saucepan of salted water to the boil. Put the pasta into the water and stir thoroughly. Replace the lid and return to the boil. Remove or adjust the lid once the water is boiling again. Cook according to the packet instructions until al dente. Drain the pasta, and return to the pot. Toss the sauce through the pasta, and serve immediately.

*Serves 4*

# spaghetti with clams

see variations page 65

Please do make sure the vongole are as clean as possible before you cook them to avoid an unpleasant muddy taste or a gritty sensation under your teeth. Rinse them in several changes of clean, fresh water until the water runs clear.

3 lbs fresh, live, baby clams, cleaned and
   scrubbed
6 tbsp. extra-virgin olive oil
3 cloves garlic, peeled and chopped finely

14 oz. spaghetti or vermicelli
Salt and freshly ground black pepper
3 tbsp. fresh flat-leaf parsley, chopped

Clean the clams really thoroughly in several changes of fresh water to make sure you have removed all traces of sand or mud. Drain the cleaned clams and put them in a wide, fairly deep skillet with 2–3 tablespoons of the oil. Cover and heat. When the skillet is very hot, shake it regularly over the heat to help the clams open up. After about 8 minutes, discard any closed clams, drain the rest, reserving the liquid. Heat the remaining oil with the garlic for a few minutes, then add the clams and strain over the reserved liquid. Mix everything together and bring to the boil, then cover and take off the heat.

Bring a large saucepan of salted water to the boil. Put the pasta into the water and stir thoroughly. Replace the lid and return to the boil. Remove or adjust the lid once the water is boiling again. Cook according to the packet instructions until al dente. Drain the pasta, and return to the pot. Pour over the clams and toss everything together. Add the parsley and plenty of freshly ground black pepper, toss again, and serve immediately.

*Serves 4*

# pasta with genoese pesto

see variations page 67

This is the classic way to serve this popular green sauce, with green beans and potatoes as well as pasta. It is not usual to serve extra cheese at the table with pesto.

3 or 4 large handfuls fresh basil, gently washed
    but not bruised, dried carefully
Large pinch coarse salt
2 or 3 cloves garlic, peeled and cut in half
Generous handful pine kernels
2 to 6 tbsp. grated aged pecorino cheese
5 fl oz. best-quality olive oil

Salt and freshly ground black pepper
1 cup fresh green beans, trimmed and boiled or
    steamed until tender
1 cup potatoes, peeled, cubed, and boiled or
    steamed until tender
8 oz. trenette or linguine

Make the pesto: Put the basil, salt, and garlic into a mortar and grind to a smooth green puree. Add the pine kernels and cheese and blend these in also, then begin to add the oil a little at a time, until you have a smooth, creamy texture. Season with salt and pepper. If using a food processor, add the ingredients in the same order. Taste as you go along and adjust the quantities according to your preference.

Bring a large saucepan of salted water to the boil. Put the pasta into the water and stir thoroughly. Replace the lid and return to the boil. Remove or adjust the lid once the water is boiling again. Cook according to the packet instructions until al dente.

Drain the pasta, and return to the pot. Dress with the pesto, adding a little hot water from the pasta to help it coat all the other ingredients. Serve immediately.

*Serves 4*

# pasta with four-cheese sauce

see variations page 67

The skill of this sauce lies in getting the balance of the four cheeses right, so that you can taste the four individual flavors, rather than it tasting like a simple cheese sauce.

1 1/2 cups (12 fl. oz) light or whipping cream
1/3 cup (2 oz.) ripe Gorgonzola cheese
1/3 cup (2 oz.) fontina cheese
1/3 cup (2 oz.) Gruyère or Emmenthal cheese
1/3 cup (1 oz.) Parmesan cheese, grated

1/2 cup milk
Freshly ground black pepper
2 free-range egg yolks
2 2/3 cups (14 oz.) pasta of your choice

Pour the cream into a heatproof bowl and set it over a pan of simmering water to heat. Remove and discard the rinds from all of the soft cheeses, and cube. Put all the cheese into the cream to melt, stirring gently and frequently.

When the cheese is all melted into the cream, take it off the heat and slacken it with the milk to make the texture easier to distribute through the pasta. Add freshly ground black pepper to taste and mix in the egg yolks.

Bring a large saucepan of salted water to the boil. Put the pasta into the water and stir thoroughly. Replace the lid and return to the boil. Remove or adjust the lid once the water is boiling again. Cook according to the packet instructions until al dente. Drain the pasta, and return to the pot. Pour over the sauce, mix together thoroughly, and serve immediately.

*Serves 4*

# traditional lasagne

see variations page 68

This is one of the best-loved and much-imitated of all Italian pasta dishes.

1 onion, peeled and chopped
1 carrot, scraped and chopped
1 stick celery, chopped
Pinch dried marjoram
1/2 cup (2 oz.) dried porcini mushrooms, soaked in hot water until soft, then drained and chopped
3 tbsp. olive oil
8 oz. stewing veal, minced coarsely
2 oz. prosciutto crudo, chopped,

1 tbsp. all-purpose flour
1 large glass red wine
1/4 tsp. freshly ground nutmeg
1 1/2 cups (12 fl. oz.) thick passata
4 oz. chicken livers, cleaned and sautéed in butter until just browned, and thinly sliced
1 x quantity fresh pasta, cut into 4 x 5-in. rectangles, and blanched (page 19)
2 1/4 cups béchamel sauce (page 28)
1 cup freshly grated Parmesan cheese

Fry the vegetables and mushrooms together gently in a large pot with the oil until soft, but not colored. Add the veal, and prosciutto and cook gently until browned. Add the flour and stir until it is absorbed. Raise the heat and add the red wine, stirring for a minute or two before lowering the heat and adding the nutmeg and passata. Simmer gently for about an hour, stirring occasionally. Remove from the heat, and add the chicken livers.

Butter a medium ovenproof dish and cover the bottom with a layer of pasta sheets. Cover with the meat sauce, and then a layer of béchamel sauce. Continue in this way until you have filled the dish and used up all the ingredients, ending with a layer of pasta covered with a generous sprinkling of Parmesan cheese. Bake in a pre-heated oven at 350°F (180°C) until golden brown and bubbling hot. Leave to stand for at least 5 minutes before serving.

*Serves 4*

# ravioli with spinach & ricotta filling

see variations page 69

A classic combination, this is definitely worth a little effort for a special occasion.

2 lbs fresh spinach, picked over and washed in
    several changes of water
1 cup fresh ricotta cheese
Pinch grated nutmeg
Salt and freshly ground black pepper
1 1/2 cups freshly grated Parmesan cheese

1 x quantity fresh pasta, rolled out and cut into
    3-in. circles (page 19)
For the sage butter:
1 stick unsalted butter
5 leaves fresh sage, rubbed gently between your
    palms to release their flavor

Make the filling: Wilt the spinach in a dry skillet, then cool. When it is cool enough to handle, squeeze dry with your hands, then chop it finely. Mix the spinach, ricotta cheese, nutmeg, salt, pepper, and half the Parmesan cheese. Blend together with one egg.

Working with one piece of pasta at a time, drop a teaspoon of filling in the center of the circle. Fold the circle in half, encasing the filling. Seal the open edges of each semicircle with the prongs of a fork. If the dough is dry, you may need to run a moistened finger along the inside of the seam first. Continue in this way until all the dough has been used.

Bring a large saucepan of salted water to the boil. Put the ravioli in batches into the water and boil until tender and floating on the surface. Drain carefully with a slotted spoon, and arrange in a warmed serving dish. Meanwhile, melt the butter with the sage leaves until warm and golden, not browned. When all the pasta is in the serving dish, pour over the melted butter and mix carefully. Sprinkle with the rest of the cheese and serve immediately.

*Serves 4*

variations

# traditional christmas tortellini

see base recipe page 35

### traditional christmas tortellini with a game filling
Use minced guinea fowl, pheasant, pigeon, quail, or a combination of some or all of the above to give the tortellini a really rich, gamey flavor, then cook them in a rich game stock.

### raviolini in broth
Prepare the main recipe, but make tiny square ravioli rather than tortellini. Use the same filling to make the smallest possible ravioli and cook them in the broth to cook as above.

### traditional christmas tortellini in a sweet broth
Omit the cabbage and tomatoes from the broth ingredients and replace with a small head of cos lettuce, halved, and 2 halved zucchini for a sweeter flavor.

### traditional christmas tortellini with chicken
Use chicken breast instead of turkey breast for the filling and proceed as main recipe.

variations

# pasta carbonara

see base recipe page 37

### smoky carbonara
Use smoked pancetta, guanciale, or bacon to add another dimension of flavor to
this wonderful pasta dish.

### pasta carbonara with peas
Give the dish color and sweetness by adding 3/4 cup (4 oz.) fresh or frozen peas
to the pancetta once it is half cooked, then continue as before.

### spicy carbonara
Add 1/4 teaspoon of hot paprika to the beaten eggs.

### extra-rich carbonara
Use duck eggs in place of hen eggs to make this dish richer.

### mild carbonara
Substitute Parmesan cheese for the pecorino to make your carbonara taste less
piquant.

variations

# spaghettini with garlic & olive oil

see base recipe page 39

### spaghettini with garlic, olive oil & chile
Add 1 or 2 dried red chiles to the oil while it is heating with the garlic to flavor the oil and give the sauce a spicy kick. Discard the chile together with the garlic and proceed as main recipe.

### spaghettini with garlic, olive oil & anchovies
Add 1 or 2 drained anchovy fillets preserved in olive oil to the garlic and oil and dissolve into the oil over the heat for an added fishy, salty note.

### spaghettini with garlic, olive oil & rosemary
Add a sprig of fresh rosemary to the oil with the garlic and allow it to flavor and perfume the oil as it heats, then discard with the garlic and proceed as main recipe.

variations

# pasta with bacon, tomato and chile

see base recipe page 40

### pasta with pancetta, tomato & chile
Use unsmoked pancetta to give the sauce a simpler, cleaner flavor.

### pasta with bacon, tomato, chile & vinegar
Add 4 tablespoons red wine vinegar to the onion, garlic, and chile to add a slightly sharp flavor to the sauce.

### pasta with smooth bacon, tomato & chile sauce
For a smoother sauce, use passata instead of chopped canned tomatoes.

### pasta with creamy bacon, tomato & chile sauce
Add a heaped tablespoon of mascarpone to the sauce at the end to make it creamy.

variations

# penne arrabiata

see base recipe page 43

### fresh chile arrabiata
Use finely chopped fresh chiles instead of dried to give the sauce quite a different taste.

### smoky arrabiata
Add 1/2 teaspoon of smoked paprika to the garlic and chiles to give the sauce a lovely smoky depth.

### smooth arrabiata
Use passata instead of canned, chopped tomatoes to make the sauce really smooth.

### mild arrabiata
Leave the garlic whole and discard it with the chiles for a milder flavor.

### extra-hot arrabiata
Seed and chop the chiles very finely and leave them in the sauce to make it more fiery.

variations

# la puttanesca

see base recipe page 44

### extra-garlicky puttanesca
Puree the garlic to add a stronger garlic flavor to the sauce.

### smooth puttanesca
Use black olive paste instead of chopped whole olives for a smooth olive taste.

### sour puttanesca
Add 2 tablespoons of strong white wine vinegar to add a stronger sour note to the sauce.

### fresh puttanesca
Use chopped fresh chile instead of dried for a different taste.

### puttanesca with sardines
Use drained and flaked, canned sardines in olive oil instead of anchovies for a more pronounced fishy flavor.

variations

# bolognese ragu

see base recipe page 47

### white ragu
Leave out the tomato puree and use white wine instead of red wine (if using) to make a white ragu, finished off with the cream.

### aromatic ragu
Add a small pinch of ground cinnamon to the meat at the beginning, when browning, to add a mild spice note to the sauce.

### bolognese ragu (without the chicken livers)
Omit the chicken livers altogether for a lighter, less rich sauce.

### luxurious bolognese ragu
For extra luxury, add shaved black or white truffle to the finished sauce just before tossing through the pasta.

variations

# spaghetti with clams

see base recipe page 48

### spicy spaghetti with clams
Add half a finely chopped dried red chile pepper to the oil and garlic to give the dish a spicy note.

### spaghetti with clams & rosemary
Add 1/2 tablespoon finely chopped fresh rosemary leaves to the oil and garlic.

### spaghetti with white wine & clams
Add a glass of dry white wine to the clams while they are steaming to give a delicious wine note to the finished dish.

### spaghetti with clams & lemon
Add the finely grated zest of 1/2 an unwaxed lemon to the pasta and clams when you toss everything together for a deliciously tangy, fresh taste.

### spaghetti with mussels
Use mussels instead of clams to ring the changes — proceed exactly as above, allowing a little more time for the mussels to steam open and remove from their shells before mixing with the spaghetti.

variations

# pasta with genoese pesto

see base recipe page 51

### pasta with creamy pesto
Add 3 tablespoons of crème fraiche or sour cream to the pesto before using it to dress the pasta for a deliciously creamy dish.

### pasta with pesto
Omit the green beans and potatoes if you prefer.

### pasta with pesto & cherry tomatoes
Omit the potatoes and green beans and add a handful of roughly chopped cherry tomatoes instead.

### pasta with extra-green pesto
Use half flat-leaf parsley leaves and half basil leaves to make the pesto for a really vivid green sauce.

### pasta with parmesan cheese pesto
For a smoother tasting sauce, use freshly grated Parmesan cheese instead of pecorino.

variations

# pasta with four-cheese sauce

see base recipe page 52

### pasta with mild four-cheese sauce
Use Taleggio, rind removed, instead of Gorgonzola, for a different, less piquant taste.

### pasta with four-cheese sauce & truffles
For extra luxury, shave a small black or white truffle over the pasta just before serving, once you have tossed it with the sauce.

### pasta with rich four-cheese sauce
To make the sauce extra rich, melt the cheese into heavy cream instead of whipping cream.

### pasta with four-cheese & nutmeg sauce
Stir 1/2 teaspoon of freshly grated nutmeg to the sauce once all the cheese has melted to add a subtle spice flavor to the dish.

### pasta with four-cheese sauce & pancetta
Finish off the dish, once the pasta and sauce have been combined, with a scattering of 4 ounces crisply fried pancetta cubes just before serving.

variations

# traditional lasagne

see base recipe page 55

### luxurious lasagne
For added decadence add a small black or white truffle to the lasagne together with the cooked chicken livers.

### traditional lasagne with beef
Use stewing beef steak instead of veal and proceed as main recipe.

### traditional lasagne with pork
Use pork loin instead of veal and proceed as main recipe.

### traditional lasagne without mushrooms
Omit the dried porcini mushrooms and proceed as main recipe.

### traditional lasagne with sage
Use a pinch of dried sage instead of the dried marjoram for a different herby flavor, and proceed as main recipe.

# ravioli with spinach & ricotta filling

see base recipe page 56

### ravioli with ricotta cheese & lemon
Omit the spinach and use the ricotta cheese on its own, using 1/2 teaspoon of lemon zest instead of the nutmeg to add flavor.

### ravioli with nutty sage butter
Dress the cooked ravioli with sage butter that has been allowed to darken slightly to give it a more nutty flavor, and add a handful of pine kernels to the butter while it melts to add crunch.

### ravioli in tomato sauce
Instead of dressing the pasta with sage butter, use one of the tomato sauces on pages 22, 25 and 26 instead.

### ravioli with chard, cinnamon & ricotta cheese
Make the filling more robust in flavor by using chard instead of spinach and substituting cinnamon for the nutmeg and proceed as main recipe.

### green ravioli with ricotta cheese
Make the pasta green, by adding pureed spinach to the dough, and use a plain ricotta cheese filling to create a color contrast.

# pasta soups & salads

Perfect for a filling lunch, pick one of these tasty

soups or salads to keep you going all afternoon.

The salads are ideal for lunch boxes and picnics too

— just remember to pack a fork.

# pasta soup with potato

see variations page 90

Like all very simple recipes, this soup relies on the highest quality ingredients for the best results. For example, make sure the vegetable stock you use is packed with flavor.

1 onion, peeled
1 carrot, peeled
1 stick celery, strings removed
4 tbsp. extra-virgin olive oil
1 1/2 lbs. potatoes, peeled and sliced thickly
3 tbsp. fresh flat-leaf parsley, chopped

1 cup (8 oz.) canned tomatoes, mashed
7 cups (3 pints) vegetable stock
1 1/4 cups (5 oz.) small soup pasta
2 oz. freshly grated Parmesan cheese
Extra-virgin olive oil for drizzling

Chop the onion, carrot, and celery together and fry them gently in the olive oil until softened slightly. Add the potatoes and the parsley and mix together for a few minutes to coat with the vegetables and the oil, then add the tomatoes, stir and pour over the stock. Cover and bring to the boil, then turn down the heat and simmer very gently for about 30 minutes or until the potatoes are completely soft.

Add the pasta and simmer until cooked, making sure there is enough liquid to cook the pasta. Season and serve as soon as the pasta is tender, sprinkled with Parmesan cheese and drizzled with a final spoonful of extra-virgin olive oil.

*Serves 4*

# pasta & bean soup

see variations page 91

This is my own version of this classic "pasta e fagioli," for which literally dozens of recipes exist all over Italy.

1 1/2 cups (12 oz.) dried or 1 1/4 cups (12 oz.) canned borlotti beans
2 oz. fatty pancetta or prosciutto
3 tbsp. olive oil
1 onion, chopped
1 large carrot, chopped
1 large celery stick, chopped

4 1/4 cups (2 1/4 pints) good meat or vegetable stock
2/3 cup (2 oz.) small soup pasta
Salt and freshly ground black pepper
Extra-virgin olive oil, to serve
Parmesan cheese, to serve

If using dried beans, soak overnight in cold water, then drain and rinse. Boil quickly in salted water for 5 minutes, then drain and rinse again. Cover with fresh water and simmer gently until tender, about 40 minutes. Drain and set aside. If using canned beans, drain and set aside.

Having prepared the beans, heat the olive oil in a large pot, and gently fry the pancetta onion, carrot, and celery until the vegetables are all soft. Add the beans and stir. Add the stock and simmer slowly until the beans are almost falling apart. Add the pasta and cook until tender. Season to taste and serve warm, drizzled with a little extra-virgin olive oil and with a light sprinkling of freshly grated Parmesan cheese.

*Serves 4*

# pasta soup with lentils

see variations page 92

This is a real winter warmer, deliciously satisfying and packed with flavor. A truly lovely, traditional, rustic pasta soup.

3 tbsp. extra-virgin olive oil
6 1/2 oz. pancetta (or thick-cut bacon), coarsely
    chopped
1 small onion, finely chopped
1 small carrot, finely chopped
2 sticks celery, strings removed and finely
    chopped
2 1/2 pints (6 1/4 cups) water

1 1/4 cups passata
2 fresh rosemary sprigs, leaves picked
1/4 tsp. dried chile flakes
2 cups (8 oz.) small soup pasta
2 (14-oz.) cans lentils
2 oz. freshly grated aged and peppery pecorino
    cheese
Extra-virgin olive oil, for drizzling

Heat the oil in a large saucepan over high heat. Stir in the pancetta or bacon, onion, carrot, and celery for 5 minutes or until the vegetables are soft. Add the water, passata, rosemary, and chile flakes. Bring to the boil and simmer for about 10 minutes. Add the pasta and cook, stirring often, for 10 minutes or until the pasta is al dente. Stir the drained lentils into the soup. Cook gently, stirring occasionally, for 5 minutes or until warmed through, season to taste with salt. Top with the pecorino cheese and a drizzle of olive oil and serve.

*Serves 4*

# pasta soup with chickpeas

see variations page 93

This is said to be the oldest recorded recipe for a pasta dish; it was prepared by Roman Legionnaires over their camp fires, mixing boiled chickpeas with a primitive form of pappardelle, olive oil, and generous slug of garum, a fermented fish sauce.

9 cloves garlic, peeled and chopped to a puree
9 tbsp. olive oil
1 1/2 cups (14 oz.) canned chickpeas
2 x 2-in. sprigs fresh rosemary
2 cups (8 oz.) small soup pasta

6 salted anchovy fillets, boned, rinsed, and
    chopped very finely
2 tbsp. tomato puree
Extra-virgin olive oil, to serve
Freshly ground black pepper, to serve

In a large, deep saucepan, fry half the garlic with about one third of the oil for about 5 minutes. Add the chickpeas to the saucepan and stir together with the garlic and oil until heated through. Then add enough cold water to cover, and add the rosemary. Stir, season with salt and pepper, and cover. Leave to simmer for about 20 minutes or until the chickpeas are becoming slightly mushy. As soon as the chickpeas are mushy add the pasta to the soup, adding a little hot water if necessary. Simmer until the pasta is just tender.

While the soup is simmering, put the remaining garlic and oil in a separate small pan with the anchovy fillets and the tomato puree. Fry together very gently, stirring frequently until the garlic is soft and the mixture comes together (about 3–4 minutes). Remove from the heat and keep warm. When the pasta in the soup is cooked, stir in the anchovy and garlic mixture. Serve immediately with a little olive oil and a touch more black pepper.

*Serves 6–8*

# minestrone

see variations page 94

Minestrone is a beloved classic soup of northern Italy, for which countless recipes exist. This is my own version, made substantial by adding pasta to the vegetables and beans. In my opinion, this soup is best served warm rather than boiling hot.

2 1/2 pints (6 1/4 cups) warm vegetable stock
4 tbsp. olive oil
1 onion, peeled and chopped finely
2 sticks celery, strings removed and chopped
3/4 cup (7 oz.) canned borlotti beans, drained
4 tbsp. fresh flat-leaf parsley, chopped
10 oz. mixed green vegetables, for example:
    spinach, cabbage, Swiss chard, lettuce leaves
    or spring greens, chopped

2 zucchini, cubed
1 potato, peeled and cubed
1 small carrot, cubed
2 cups (8 oz.) small soup pasta
Salt and pepper
2 or 3 tbsp. freshly grated Parmesan cheese,
    to serve
Extra-virgin olive oil, to serve

In a large, deep saucepan, fry the onion and celery gently in the olive oil until soft. Add the borlotti beans and stir together thoroughly. Then add the parsley, green vegetables, zucchini, potato, and carrot. Fry together gently, using a little of the stock to moisten. When the vegetables are all beginning to soften, add the rest of the stock, turn the heat down, and simmer slowly for about 30 minutes, stirring regularly. Add more liquid if necessary.

When the vegetables are completely soft, season to taste and add the pasta. Simmer gently until the pasta is cooked. Remove from the heat, allow to stand for about 10 minutes before serving with a little freshly grated Parmesan cheese and a drizzle of extra-virgin olive oil.

*Serves 4*

# tomato, mozzarella & basil pasta salad

see variations page 95

This fresh, summery, and colorful dish is one of the most delicious ways of serving pasta. Only make this in summer with the very best ripe and juicy tomatoes.

8 large, ripe tomatoes, peeled and seeded
1 clove garlic, peeled and ground to a puree
2 tbsp. fresh flat-leaf parsley, chopped
12 large leaves basil, torn into pieces with your
    fingers

Salt and freshly ground black pepper
8 tbsp. extra-virgin olive oil
2 2/3 cups (14 oz.) short pasta of your choice
1 fresh mozzarella cheese, cubed

Chop the tomatoes roughly and put them into a large bowl with the garlic, parsley, basil, and seasoning. Stir in the oil and leave to stand, covered, for at least an hour.

Bring a large saucepan of salted water to the boil. Put the pasta into the water and stir thoroughly. Replace the lid and return to the boil. Remove or adjust the lid once the water is boiling again. Cook according to the packet instructions until al dente. Drain and add to the bowl of tomatoes, and add the mozzarella. Mix together and serve at once.

# conchiglie with avocado & ricotta

see variations page 96

This pasta dish is dressed with a lovely pale green sauce that requires no cooking at all. Ideal for hot summer days. The seashell shape of the pasta (conchiglie means shells) holds the sauce perfectly.

2 2/3 cups (14 oz.) conchiglie
2 ripe avocados, peeled and mashed
7 tbsp. fresh ricotta cheese
2 tbsp. milk or half and half

Salt and freshly ground black pepper
1 tbsp. fresh flat-leaf parsley, chopped
Freshly grated Parmesan cheese, to serve

Bring a large saucepan of salted water to the boil. Put the pasta into the water and stir thoroughly. Replace the lid and return to the boil. Remove or adjust the lid once the water is boiling again. Cook according to the packet instructions until al dente. Drain, and run under cold water until the pasta is cool.

Meanwhile, beat the mashed avocado with the ricotta cheese and milk or half and half to make a fairly smooth sauce. Season with salt and pepper, and then stir in the parsley. Add the pasta and toss together thoroughly, adding a little water if required. Chill for at least 2 hours before serving, and offer freshly grated Parmesan cheese separately.

*Serves 4*

# pasta salad with peppers

see variations page 97

This combination of flavors is really delicious; this is definitely one of my favorite pasta salad recipes.

4 large ripe tomatoes
1 large red pepper
1 large yellow pepper
Juice of 1 lemon
Salt

7 tbsp. extra-virgin olive oil
1 tsp. Italian mustard
2 1/3 cups (12 oz.) fusilli
1 large handful fresh basil leaves, washed and
    finely chopped

Blanch the tomatoes in boiling water, then skin and seed them. Chop into rough chunks. Broil the peppers until browned. Place them in a bowl, cover with a sheet of plastic wrap to steam until completely cooled, then remove then from the bowl and skin them. Remove the seeds from the peppers and cut the flesh into rough chunks. In a small bowl, mix together the lemon juice with the salt, oil, and mustard until thickened and creamy.

Bring a large saucepan of salted water to the boil. Put the pasta into the water and stir thoroughly. Replace the lid and return to the boil. Remove or adjust the lid once the water is boiling again. Cook according to the packet instructions until al dente. Drain, and run under cold water until pasta is cool.

Transfer the pasta to a large salad bowl and add the tomatoes, peppers, and dressing. Mix together thoroughly. Add the basil and adjust seasoning. Refrigerate for at least an hour before serving.

*Serves 4*

# fusilli with arugula & tomatoes

see variations page 98

This is a wonderfully fresh tasting summer pasta salad packed with flavor and bursting with color. Really wonderful for hot days.

2 2/3 cups (14 oz.) fusilli
20 cherry tomatoes
25 black olives, de-stoned
1 large buffalo mozzarella cheese
5 cups (3 1/4 oz.) arugula, washed and dried

4 tbsp. freshly grated Parmesan cheese
6 tbsp. extra-virgin olive oil
1 heaped tsp. dried oregano
Salt and freshly ground black pepper
Extra-virgin olive oil, to serve

Bring a large saucepan of salted water to the boil. Put the pasta into the water and stir thoroughly. Replace the lid and return to the boil. Remove or adjust the lid once the water is boiling again. Cook according to the packet instructions until al dente. Drain, and run under cold water until pasta is cool.

Coarsely chop the cherry tomatoes, removing the seeds, and chop the olives. Drain and cut the mozzarella into cubes. Place the cooled pasta into a large bowl, and add the tomatoes, mozzarella, arugula, Parmesan, olive oil and oregano. Mix everything together thoroughly and refrigerate until required. Just before serving, season and add a little more olive oil, stirring well.

*Serves 4*

# fusilli with rosemary

see variations page 99

This is a very fragrant, delicate-tasting pasta dish that is so quick and easy to prepare.

2 3/4 cups (1 lb.) fusilli
5 x 4 inch sprigs fresh young rosemary, washed
    and leaves removed

1 cup light or whipping cream
1/2 cup (2 oz.) freshly grated Parmesan cheese
Salt and freshly ground black pepper

Bring a large saucepan of salted water to the boil. Put the pasta into the water and stir thoroughly. Replace the lid and return to the boil. Remove or adjust the lid once the water is boiling again. Cook according to the packet instructions until al dente. Drain, and run under cold water until pasta is cool.

While the pasta is cooking, chop the rosemary very finely. Tip the chopped rosemary into a large bowl and stir in the cream, Parmesan cheese, and seasoning. Add the cooled pasta, toss together quickly and serve at once.

*Serves 4*

variations

# pasta soup with potato

see base recipe page 71

### pasta soup with garlic & potato

Omit the onion, carrot, and celery and substitute with 2 cloves of minced, peeled garlic to give the soup a completely different, much more intense flavor.

### pasta soup with potato & rosemary

Omit the tomatoes and replace with 1 tablespoon of very finely chopped fresh, soft rosemary leaves.

### spicy pasta soup with potato

Add 1 finely chopped, seeded red chile pepper to the frying vegetables before adding the potatoes to give this soup some real heat, and sprinkle with pecorino cheese instead of Parmesan just before serving.

# pasta & bean soup

see base recipe page 73

### pasta & cannellini bean soup
Substitute 1 1/2 cups cannellini beans for the borlotti beans to change the color and flavor of this soup.

### spicy pasta & bean soup
Stir 2 teaspoons ground chile into the vegetables while they are frying, and dress the soup with a little chile oil in place of the olive oil, just before serving.

### pasta, bean & pesto soup
For a more summery version of this soup, serve at room temperature. Add a small handful of fresh basil leaves, ripped into small pieces, to the frying vegetables, and drop 1 teaspoon of fresh pesto on top of each bowl of soup just before serving.

### vegetarian pasta & bean soup
Omit the pancetta or prosciutto and replace with 2 small zucchini, cubed, and fried with the other vegetables.

### pasta & fresh bean soup
For a fresher tasting soup, omit the borlotti beans and use the same quantity of fresh or frozen green beans, chopped and then fried together with the other vegetables, omitting the pancetta or prosciutto.

variations

# pasta soup with lentils

see base recipe page 75

### vegetarian pasta soup with potatoes
Omit the pancetta or bacon and add a couple of peeled and cubed potatoes
to the vegetables at the beginning to make this soup more substantial and
suitable for vegetarians.

### pasta soup with lentils & chile oil
Drizzle the soup with a little chile oil just before serving to add even more
heat and spice.

### sweet vegetarian pasta soup with lentils
Add 2 peeled and finely chopped dessert apples to the vegetables instead of
the pancetta of bacon at the beginning of this recipe to make this soup
vegetarian-friendly and to give it a lovely sweet note. When you drizzle with
the oil at the very end, add a couple of drops of sweet and sticky balsamic
vinegar to accentuate the sweetness of the apple.

variations

# pasta soup with chickpeas

see base recipe page 76

### simple pasta soup with chickpeas & parmesan
Omit the anchovy and garlic sauce and serve the soup simply drizzled with
olive oil and sprinkled with freshly grated Parmesan cheese.

### pasta soup with chickpeas & pancetta
Sauté the softened chickpeas and garlic in the olive oil with 3 tablespoons
cubed pancetta or chopped streaky bacon to add a lovely meaty flavor to this
soup. In this instance, omit the anchovy sauce.

### pasta soup with chickpeas & chile oil
To add extra fire, finish off the soup with a generous drizzle of chile oil instead
of the oil and black pepper.

variations

# minestrone

see base recipe page 79

### bean minestrone
Omit the green vegetables completely and replace with 7 ounces green beans, topped and tailed and chopped into short sections.

### chicken minestrone
Use chicken stock instead of vegetable stock to give this lovely soup a richer taste, and add 1/2 a chicken breast, cooked and shredded, with the stock.

### minestrone with chickpeas
Substitute the borlotti beans for chickpeas.

variations

# tomato, mozzarella & basil pasta salad

see base recipe page 80

### spicy tomato, mozzarella & basil pasta salad
To add a hot note to this dish, add a finely chopped, seeded fresh chile to the tomatoes, garlic, parsley, basil, and seasoning.

### tomato, mozzarella & oregano pasta salad
Omit the parsley and the basil, and replace with 2 tablespoons of dried oregano to completely change the flavor of this delicious dish.

### hot tomato & basil pasta
Simply serve the dish before refrigerating, omitting the mozzarella.

### lemony tomato, mozzarella & basil pasta salad
To give the dish a different flavor, use lemon-flavored olive oil instead of plain olive oil to marinate the tomatoes, garlic, herbs, and seasoning.

### tomato, mozzarella, olive & basil salad
To add more flavors to the dish, add a handful of chopped black olives and a tablespoon of drained, rinsed, and roughly chopped capers to the tomatoes, garlic, herbs, seasoning, and oil.

variations

# conchiglie with avocado & ricotta

see base recipe page 83

### conchiglie with avocado, ricotta & chile
Add 1 very finely chopped fresh chile pepper (seeds removed) to the mashed avocado to create a wonderful contrast of flavors in this simple pasta salad.

### conchiglie with avocado, ricotta & sun-dried tomatoes
Prepare the basic recipe, and finish with 2 tablespoons chopped sun-dried tomatoes and 2 tablespoons toasted pine kernels sprinkled over the dish just before serving.

### conchiglie with avocado, ricotta & pancetta
Fry 1 cup cubed pancetta in a small skillet until crisp and brown, allow to cool, then sprinkle over the dressed pasta salad just before serving.

### mexican conchiglie salad
Substitute the parsley for cilantro and add 1 teaspoon of Tabasco to the mashed avocado to give the dish a slightly Mexican twist.

variations

# pasta salad with peppers

see base recipe page 85

### quick pasta salad with peppers
Use canned or bottled roasted peppers instead of roasting your own.

### pasta salad with asparagus
Substitute the peppers for 20 steamed, just-cooked asparagus spears, cut into
lengths equal to the penne, and precede as main recipe.

### pasta salad with tuna & peppers
Add a large can of tuna, flaked, to the pasta salad at the very end when
combining all the ingredients together.

### pasta salad with peppers & capers
Add 2 tablespoons small pickled capers, drained and rinsed, to the pasta salad at
the end.

### pasta salad with pesto & peppers
Add a tablespoon of fresh pesto and a handful of toasted pine kernels the salad
at the end.

variations

# fusilli with arugula & tomato

see base recipe page 87

### fusilli with arugula, tomato & avocado
After refrigeration and just before you serve this fabulous pasta salad, add 1 cubed avocado with the oil and mix through gently.

### tricolor fusilli salad
For even more color, add about 5 tablespoons canned sweet corn to the salad with the tomatoes and olives and mix through.

### fusilli with arugula, tomato & pesto
Substitute the oregano for a small handful of fresh basil leaves, torn into shreds, and mix 1 teaspoon of fresh pesto into the oil before combining everything together.

### fusilli with arugula, tomato & pine kernels
For added crunch, add 3 tablespoons toasted pine kernels to the pasta, tomatoes, and other ingredients when combining everything together.

### fusilli with arugula, tomato & asparagus
Add 20 small, freshly cooked and cooled asparagus tips to the salad together with the tomatoes and mix through gently.

# creamy fusilli salad with rosemary

see base recipe page 89

### extra-rich fusilli salad with rosemary
For some added richness, add 1 egg yolk to the cream with the other ingredients and proceed as main recipe.

### fusilli salad with mascarpone & rosemary
Substitute the cream for mascarpone, slightly slackened with a couple of tablespoon of milk, and use grated pecorino cheese instead of Parmesan to create an interesting contrast of flavors.

### creamy fusilli salad with rosemary & pancetta
Separately fry 4 ounces smoked pancetta cubes in a small skillet and scatter them over the pasta once it is dressed and ready to serve.

### creamy fusilli salad with rosemary & potato
To make this dish more substantial, add 2 medium sized potatoes, boiled and peeled, then mix them, hot, into the hot cooked pasta and cream, finish off with 1 ounce crispy bacon, crumbled.

# pasta with meat

This chapter contains delectable recipes for meat

lovers, often combined with vegetables and cheese

to create some memorable pasta dishes.

# farfalle with sausage & tomato

see variations page 124

This is one of those great, filling, and satisfying pasta sauces that taste even better when reheated the following day. Italian sausages are much coarser than many other kinds, and tend to be quite peppery.

1/2 cup dried porcini mushrooms
1 onion, peeled and chopped
3 tbsp. unsalted butter
1 lb. Italian sausages, crumbled

2 cups (10 oz.) chopped prosciutto crudo
1 cup (8 oz.) drained canned tomatoes, chopped
2 2/3 cups (14 oz.) farfalle pasta
4 tbsp. freshly grated Parmesan cheese

Soak the mushrooms in hand-hot water until softened. Fry the onion until soft in the butter, then add the sausage and prosciutto. Fry together gently for about 10 minutes, then add the tomatoes, season, and simmer for about 20 minutes.

Bring a large saucepan of salted water to the boil. Put the pasta into the water and stir thoroughly. Replace the lid and return to the boil. Remove or adjust the lid once the water is boiling again. Cook according to the packet instructions until al dente. Drain, and return to the pot. Pour over the sauce and mix together thoroughly. Add the Parmesan and stir again. Serve immediately.

*Serves 4*

# macaroni with meatballs

see variations page 125

I feel that serving meatballs with a short pasta like rigatoni or macaroni works better than the more traditional spaghetti.

1 onion, peeled and chopped
1/2 cup olive oil
1 lb. ground pork
2 eggs, beaten
Salt and freshly ground black pepper
1 clove garlic, peeled and chopped finely

Handful of fresh flat-leaf parsley, chopped
5 or 6 tbsp. fine, dry breadcrumbs
3 cups passata
Handful of mixed fresh herbs, chopped finely
3 1/3 cups (1 lb. 1 oz.) large macaroni

Fry the onion in the olive oil until softened but not browned, then take off the heat until required. Mix the pork with the eggs, seasoning, garlic, parsley, and 2 to 3 tablespoons of the breadcrumbs. With wet hands to prevent sticking, shape the mixture into meatballs about the size of large olives, roll in the remaining breadcrumbs and fry gently in the re-heated onion and oil for about 2 minutes, or until sealed and lightly browned. Drain off any excess oil and add the passata and the chopped mixed herbs. Simmer together for about an hour, stirring frequently and adding a little water if necessary.

Bring a large saucepan of salted water to the boil. Put the macaroni into the water and stir thoroughly. Replace the lid and return to the boil. Remove or adjust the lid once the water is boiling again. Cook according to the packet instructions until al dente. Drain, and return to the pot. Pour over the sauce and the meatballs, mix gently to prevent breaking up the meatballs, and serve immediately.

*Serves 6*

# pasta with pancetta & mushrooms

see variations page 126

This is a very tasty pasta dish for everyone who loves the wonderful combination of crispy pancetta or bacon with creamy mushrooms.

2 2/3 cups (14 oz.) macaroni or other chunky
    pasta shape
6 tbsp. cubed pancetta (or thick-cut bacon)
2 cups fresh mushrooms, wiped clean and thinly
    sliced
2 tbsp. unsalted butter

1 clove finely chopped garlic
3 tbsp. heavy cream
Freshly ground black pepper
3 tbsp. freshly grated Parmesan cheese
1 tbsp. fresh flat-leaf parsley, chopped

Fry the pancetta in a non-stick skillet until brown and crisp. In a separate skillet, fry the mushrooms, butter, and garlic together until the mushrooms are soft and well dried out. Stir in the cream, season with salt and pepper, remove from the heat and keep warm.

Bring a large saucepan of salted water to the boil. Put the pasta into the water and stir thoroughly. Replace the lid and return to the boil. Remove or adjust the lid once the water is boiling again. Cook according to the packet instructions until al dente. Drain, and return to the pot. Pour over the pancetta, mushroom, and cream sauce and toss together thoroughly, then add half the cheese and toss again. Transfer on to a warm platter or individual warmed plates and sprinkle with the rest of the Parmesan cheese and the parsley to serve.

*Serves 4*

# penne with pork ragu

see variations page 127

This is a perfect winter supper dish: A satisfying baked pasta dish with a lovely cheesy topping, dressed with a tasty pork ragu.

1 clove garlic, peeled and crushed
3 tbsp. extra-virgin olive oil
1 onion, peeled and finely chopped
4 oz. coarsely ground pork
1 dried bay leaf
Salt and freshly ground pepper
2 cups hot meat stock

1 (14-oz.) can tomatoes, drained and chopped
2 1/3 cups (14 oz.) penne
1 tbsp. finely chopped fresh rosemary leaves
4 tbsp. unsalted butter
3 tbsp. dried breadcrumbs
4 tbsp. freshly grated Parmesan cheese

Preheat the oven to 425°F (220°C). Fry the garlic gently in the olive oil until golden, then discard the garlic, and add the onion and cook until softened. Add the meat, cook until browned, and add the bay leaf and seasoning. Add the hot stock and the tomatoes. Stir, cover, and simmer gently for about 50 minutes.

Bring a large saucepan of salted water to the boil. Put the penne into the water and stir thoroughly. Replace the lid and return to the boil. Remove or adjust the lid once the water is boiling again. Cook according to the packet instructions until al dente. Drain, and return to the pot. Add the finely chopped rosemary leaves and the sauce. Mix together thoroughly. Butter a large ovenproof dish and transfer the pasta mixture to the dish. Sprinkle the top generously with breadcrumbs and freshly grated Parmesan cheese, and dot with the remaining butter. Bake in the oven for about 10 minutes before serving.

*Serves 4*

# bavette with roman sauce

see variations page 128

Bavette are very similar to linguine — long flattened spaghetti — and are traditionally served with this sauce, though you can use any shape of pasta you have available.

2 heaped tbsp. dried porcini mushrooms
2 cups cherry tomatoes, halved
3 tbsp. extra-virgin olive oil
1 onion, peeled and finely chopped
3 tbsp. cubed smoked pancetta

10 oz. bavette (or linguine)
3 tbsp. freshly grated grana padano cheese
2 tbsp. unsalted butter
Salt and freshly ground black pepper
Handful of fresh flat-leaf parsley, chopped

Soak the mushrooms in hand-hot water for about 30 minutes. Remove the seeds from the tomatoes with a teaspoon, and then chop them finely. In a medium skillet, warm the oil and fry the onion and pancetta until the pancetta is crisp and the onion is a pale golden brown. Drain the mushrooms, reserving the liquid. Roughly chop the mushrooms, then add to the pancetta and onions, mix together and add the tomatoes. Season with salt and pepper, add the liquid from the mushrooms, and simmer for 25 minutes.

Bring a large saucepan of salted water to the boil. Put the penne into the water and stir thoroughly. Replace the lid and return to the boil. Remove or adjust the lid once the water is boiling again. Cook according to the packet instructions until al dente. Drain, and return to the pot. Add the sauce to the pasta and mix together over a low heat for about 5 minutes, adding the grated cheese and the butter. Serve at once, sprinkled with the chopped parsley.

*Serves 4*

# pennette with salame

see variations page 129

Pennette are small penne, and I think they are the best shape for this dish. Alternatively, a small shape like orecchiette or mini fusilli would also work well.

2 tbsp. unsalted butter
4 oz. soft Italian salame, peeled and chopped
1/2 cup dry white wine
1 tbsp. concentrated tomato puree

Salt and freshly ground black pepper
2 2/3 cups (14 oz.) pennette
4 tbsp. freshly grated Parmesan cheese

Fry the butter and salame together gently until browned, then add the wine and the tomato puree. Season, stir, and simmer gently for about 5 minutes.

Bring a large saucepan of salted water to the boil. Put the pennette into the water and stir thoroughly. Replace the lid and return to the boil. Remove or adjust the lid once the water is boiling again. Cook according to the packet instructions until al dente. Drain, and return to the pot. Add the sauce and mix together thoroughly, making sure the sauce is evenly distributed through the pasta. Serve immediately, sprinkled with the Parmesan cheese.

*Serves 4*

# beef cannelloni

see variations page 130

The pasta for this traditional dish is much coarser than ordinary fresh pasta. If you prefer a more delicate kind of pasta, refer to the making fresh pasta instructions on page 19.

3 cups (13 oz.) all-purpose flour
1 1/4 cups (7 oz.) fine polenta flour
5 eggs
4 tbsp. extra-virgin olive oil
14 oz. lean ground beef

6 tbsp. freshly grated Parmesan cheese
1 pinch freshly grated nutmeg
Salt & freshly ground black pepper
2 tbsp. unsalted butter
1 egg yolk, beaten

Preheat the oven to 300°F (150°C). Knead the flours together with three of the eggs, a pinch of salt, and enough water to make solid but elastic dough. Roll the dough out thinly and cut it into rectangular pasta sheets. Bring a large saucepan of salted water to the boil, and add the pasta sheets for just 2 minutes before draining and refreshing in cold water. Store them in a shallow tray in cold water with 1 tablespoon of extra-virgin olive oil to prevent them from sticking until required.

Meanwhile, brown the beef with the remaining olive oil in a separate pan, remove from the heat, tip into a bowl, and cool. Once cooled, add the remaining eggs, half the Parmesan cheese, nutmeg, and seasoning, and mix together. Butter a medium ovenproof dish thoroughly. Drain the pasta sheets one at a time, blot dry, and fill each one with some of the meat mixture. Roll up and place side by side in the ovenproof dish. Dot with the butter, brush with the beaten egg yolk, and sprinkle with the remaining Parmesan cheese. Bake in the oven for 35 minutes or until browned. Let stand for 10 minutes before serving.

*Serves 4*

# pasta al forno

see variations page 131

This is a simple and easy dish that I often fondly remember enjoying during my childhood in Tuscany. I really prefer to use penne when I make this as it fits my memories much better, but conchiglie or macaroni work too.

2 2/3 cups (14 oz.) pasta (penne or macaroni)
1 quantity béchamel sauce (see page 28)
6 tbsp. freshly grated Parmesan cheese
8 oz. cooked ham, chopped

3 tbsp. unsalted butter
salt and freshly ground black pepper

Bring a large saucepan of salted water to the boil. Put the pennette into the water and stir thoroughly. Replace the lid and return to the boil. Remove or adjust the lid once the water is boiling again. Cook according to the packet instructions until al dente. Drain, and return to the pot.

Meanwhile, heat through the sauce and melt two thirds of the Parmesan into it. Add two thirds of the sauce and all of the ham. Mix together. Grease a large ovenproof dish with half the butter. Pour in the dressed pasta and arrange it evenly in a thick layer.

Pour over the remaining sauce and dot with the remaining butter. Sprinkle with the remaining Parmesan. Bake in a preheated oven at 375°F (190°C) for about 15 minutes or until golden and bubbling. Remove from the oven, rest for 5 minutes, and then serve.

*Serves 4*

# tagliatelle with chicken livers

see variations page 132

Like all recipes that contain very few ingredients, this recipe relies heavily on the quality and freshness of the chicken livers to make it taste special.

5 oz. fresh chicken livers
4 tbsp. unsalted butter
6 tbsp. rich chicken stock
12 oz. tagliatelle

4 tbsp. freshly grated Parmesan cheese
Salt and freshly ground black pepper
2 tbsp. fresh flat-leaf parsley, chopped

Clean and trim the chicken livers, removing all traces of bile, and chop roughly. In a very large saucepan, quickly fry the butter and chicken livers together. As soon as they are well browned, add the stock and remove from the heat.

Bring a large saucepan of salted water to the boil. Put the pennette into the water and stir thoroughly. Replace the lid and return to the boil. Remove or adjust the lid once the water is boiling again. Cook according to the packet instructions until al dente. Drain, and transfer to the pot with the cooked chicken livers and mix thoroughly together. Season, stir the Parmesan cheese through the mixture, and serve sprinkled with the chopped parsley.

*Serves 4*

# spaghetti bolognese

see variations page 133

The most important ingredient in this dish is quite simply time — this is not a sauce that likes to be rushed, and is better still if allowed to rest for at least 2 hours before being re-heated and served.

6 tbsp. olive or vegetable oil
1 onion, peeled and finely chopped
1 carrot, scraped and finely chopped
2 sticks celery, finely chopped
3 cloves garlic, minced
2 tbsp. finely chopped pancetta
1 lb. lean ground beef

1 large glass red wine
1 tbsp. tomato puree diluted with 1/2 cup water
1 1/2 cups passata
Salt and freshly ground black pepper
14 oz. spaghetti
5 tbsp. freshly grated Parmesan cheese, to serve

Heat the oil and fry the onion, carrot, celery, and garlic together until the onion is soft and transparent. Add the pancetta, stir and simmer for about 5 minutes, and add the beef. Brown the beef carefully, without letting it go crisp, then pour in the wine and raise the heat to evaporate the alcohol. Pour in the diluted tomato puree and the passata. Stir carefully. Season to taste and cover. Simmer very, very gently for about 2 hours, adding water or stock if necessary and stirring frequently.

Bring a large saucepan of salted water to the boil. Put the spaghetti into the water and stir thoroughly. Replace the lid and return to the boil. Remove or adjust the lid once the water is boiling again. Cook according to the packet instructions until al dente. If you have rested the sauce, reheat it now until hot. Drain the pasta, and return to the pot, add the sauce and mix together thoroughly and sprinkle with freshly grated Parmesan cheese and serve at once.

*Serves 4*

# ruote with pea & sausage sauce

see variations page 134

Ruote are wheels of pasta, with grooves that perfectly trap the peas and sausages in this deliciously filling dish.

4 tbsp. olive oil
1 large onion, peeled and chopped finely
2 cups frozen or fresh, podded peas
4 large fresh Italian sausages

5 tbsp. heavy cream
Salt and freshly ground black pepper
2 2/3 cups (14 oz.) ruote
3 tbsp. freshly grated Parmesan cheese

Gently fry the onion in the oil in a large skillet until soft, but not browned, then add the peas and a little water. Simmer gently, adding water to the peas to prevent them drying out. Peel and crumble the sausages and add to the peas. Cook together, stirring occasionally until the sausages are well browned and the peas soft. Stir the cream into the peas and sausages, remove from the heat, and keep warm.

Bring a large saucepan of salted water to the boil. Put the ruote into the water and stir thoroughly. Replace the lid and return to the boil. Remove or adjust the lid once the water is boiling again. Cook according to the packet instructions until al dente. Drain, and return to the pot, tip in the sausage and pea sauce and mix together thoroughly. Sprinkle with the grated Parmesan cheese and serve immediately.

*Serves 4*

# macaroni with prosciutto

see variations page 135

This is a deliciously quick and easy pasta dish, perfect for a speedy supper solution.
Grana Padano is very similar to Parmesan cheese — substitute this if you can't find it.

4 tbsp. unsalted butter
3 leaves fresh sage, washed and finely chopped
1 sprig fresh rosemary, leaves removed and
    finely chopped

3/4 cup chopped prosciutto crudo
Freshly ground black pepper
2 2/3 cups (14 oz.) macaroni
3 tbsp. freshly grated Grana Padano cheese

Melt the butter in small pan with the sage and rosemary; as soon as it is sizzling hot, add the
prosciutto and some freshly ground black pepper.

Bring a large saucepan of salted water to the boil. Put the macaroni into the water and stir
thoroughly. Replace the lid and return to the boil. Remove or adjust the lid once the water is
boiling again. Cook according to the packet instructions until al dente. Drain the pasta,
reserving a little of the cooking water, and return to the pot. Add the ham and herb mixture.
Mix together, adding the grated Grana Padano and a little of the water in which the pasta
was cooked. Remove the herbs and serve immediately, offering extra Grana Padano
separately at the table.

*Serves 4*

# pasta with mortadella

see variations page 136

Another quick and easy pasta dish that requires very little preparation, and is really delicious and satisfying. Perfect for a simple family meal.

2 2/3 cups (14 oz.) short pasta (such as fusilli)
4 tbsp. unsalted butter
3/4 cup (6 oz.) grated Gruyère cheese

1 cup chopped mortadella
Freshly ground black pepper

Bring a large saucepan of salted water to the boil. Put the pasta into the water and stir thoroughly. Replace the lid and return to the boil. Remove or adjust the lid once the water is boiling again. Cook according to the packet instructions until al dente. Meanwhile, put the butter, Gruyère, and mortadella into a wide bowl and mix together. Drain the pasta, and tip it over the butter, Gruyère cheese, and mortadella. Quickly mix these together. Finish with a little freshly ground black pepper just before serving.

*Serves 4*

# penne with leeks, speck & gorgonzola

see variations page 137

This is one of those recipes that seems to me to welcome the first chilly days of fall, and certainly helps to cheer me up as the days grow shorter and the days grayer. This is a very substantial dish, so you could serve it with just a salad on the side.

1 large leek
4 tbsp. extra-virgin olive oil
2 2/3 cups (14 oz.) penne

1/4 cup (4 oz.) sweet, ripe Gorgonzola cheese
3 oz. thick-cut speck
Ground white pepper

Trim and wash the leek, then slice it into thin rounds. Heat the oil gently in a large pan and add the leek, fry gently until softened and slightly caramelized, adding a little water if necessary. Cut the speck into strips and then add the speck to the leeks, stir and continue to cook gently together. When the leeks are softened, remove from the heat and add the Gorgonzola to the pan and stir through until the cheese has melted completely.

Bring a large saucepan of salted water to the boil. Put the pasta into the water and stir thoroughly. Replace the lid and return to the boil. Remove or adjust the lid once the water is boiling again. Cook according to the packet instructions until al dente. Drain, and add to the pan with the leeks, speck, and Gorgonzola. Toss everything together and season with white pepper before serving.

*Serves 4*

variations

# farfalle with sausage & tomato sauce

see base recipe page 101

### farfalle with quick sausage & tomato sauce
To cook the sauce more quickly, use passata instead of canned chopped tomatoes.

### farfalle with garlicky sausage & tomato sauce
For a different taste, use 3 cloves finely chopped peeled cloves of garlic instead of the onion.

### farfalle with rich sausage & tomato sauce
Use bacon instead of the prosciutto crudo for a richer tasting sauce with a different texture.

### farfalle with sausage, tomato & rosemary sauce
Add a tablespoon of finely chopped fresh rosemary leaves to the onion to add another flavor dimension.

### farfalle with sausage & tomato sauce with pecorino cheese
Use grated, aged pecorino cheese instead of Parmesan to finish off the dish when you toss everything together.

variations

# macaroni with meatballs

see base recipe page 102

### macaroni with beefy meatballs
Use minced beef instead of minced pork to make the sauce taste different.

### macaroni with pork & prosciutto meatballs
For extra flavor, and 3 or 4 slices of finely chopped prosciutto crudo to the minced pork and then proceed as for main recipe.

### macaroni with zesty meatballs
For a tangy flavor, add 2 teaspoons of finely grated unwaxed lemon zest to the minced pork mixture.

### macaroni with garlicky meatballs
If you love garlic, add a finely minced clove or two of garlic to the minced pork mixture then proceed as before.

### macaroni with spicy meatballs
Add 1 teaspoon ground chile to the pork mixture, and then proceed as for main recipe.

variations

# pasta with pancetta & mushrooms

see base recipe page 105

### pasta with pancetta & porcini mushrooms
Instead of fresh mushrooms, use a large handful of dried porcini mushrooms, soaked in hand-hot water for 30 minutes, then drained and chopped for a richer, denser taste.

### pasta with smoky bacon & mushrooms
Use chopped smoked streaky bacon instead of pancetta for a deliciously smoky flavor.

### pasta with pancetta, mushrooms & sage
Add a tablespoon of finely chopped fresh sage leaves to the mushrooms while you fry them off to give the dish a lovely herby taste.

### pasta with pancetta, mushrooms & mascarpone
Use mascarpone instead of heavy cream to add a different creamy flavor to the dish.

### pasta with white wine, pancetta & mushrooms
Add a small glass of white wine or dry sherry to the frying mushrooms to add a deliciously grown-up flavor to the dish.

variations

# penne with pork ragu

see base recipe page 106

### penne tossed with pork ragu
Instead of baking the pasta, you could also just toss the sauce, pasta, and Parmesan cheese together, omitting the butter and the breadcrumbs.

### penne with beef sauce
Use beef instead of pork for a different sauce.

### penne with roman sauce & sage
Omit the rosemary and use finely chopped fresh sage instead to make the sauce taste quite different.

### penne with roman sauce with pepper
Add a diced red pepper to the meat while you brown it for extra flavor and texture.

### penne with sweet & sour roman sauce
Sprinkle 2 teaspoons of balsamic vinegar over the pork while browning it to add a sweet and sour note to the dish.

variations

# bavette with roman sauce

see base recipe page 109

### bavette with peas & pancetta
Omit the mushrooms and add 5 tablespoons fresh or frozen peas instead,
added to the onion and pancetta, and then proceed as main recipe.

### bavette with garlicky roman sauce
To completely change the flavor of this sauce, omit the onion and use
3 cloves peeled garlic, finely minced, instead.

### bavette with smoky roman sauce
To make the sauce taste even smokier, add 1/2 teaspoon smoked cayenne
to the pan with the mushrooms.

### bavette with mild roman sauce
For a milder tasting sauce, omit the smoked pancetta and replace with finely
chopped prosciutto crudo.

### bavette with smooth roman sauce
For a smoother sauce, replace the cherry tomatoes with 10 fluid ounces
(1 1/4 cups) thick passata.

variations

# pennette with salame

see base recipe page 110

### pennette with spicy salame
To make this spicy, use a Salame Napoletano or Calabrese, both of which traditionally contain chile.

### pennette with pancetta
Omit the salame and use cubed pancetta instead.

### pennette with salame & peas
Add 1 cup peas to the butter and salame to add color and sweetness to the dish.

### pennette with salame & ricotta cheese
Add 2 tablespoons ricotta cheese to the pasta and sauce when mixing them together to add texture and flavor.

### pennette with salame & sage
Add 3 teaspoons finely washed and dried chopped sage leaves to the salame and butter when frying together to add a herby flavor.

variations

# beef cannelloni

see base recipe page 111

### pork & sage cannelloni
Substitute the minced beef with coarsely minced pork and continue as above, adding a pinch of dried sage leaves to the meat as it browns.

### turkey liver cannelloni
Substitute the minced beef with minced turkey and add 3 ounces of cleaned and sliced turkey or chicken livers, fried with the mince for the last 3 or 4 minutes of the cooking time, then proceed as main recipe.

### beef cannelloni with truffle
For added luxury, shave a small black truffle over the dish as soon as it comes out of the oven.

### beef & mushroom cannelloni
Add 2 handfuls of thinly sliced mushrooms to the mince while it cooks and use freshly grated pecorino cheese instead of Parmesan, then proceed as main recipe.

### beef & spinach cannelloni
Add 3 handfuls fresh baby spinach, washed and drained, to the minced beef as it cooks, stirring it through as it wilts and the beef browns. Once combined and cooked, proceed as main recipe.

variations

# pasta al forno

see base recipe page 113

### pasta al forno with peas & emmenthal
Add 1/2 cup cooked peas and 1/2 cup cubed Emmenthal to the pasta sauce with the ham and mix together before proceeding as main recipe.

### pasta al forno with zucchini & mozzarella
Add 1/2 cup cubed, sautéed zucchini and 2/3 cup shredded mozzarella to the pasta sauce with the ham and mix together before proceeding as main recipe.

### smoky pasta al forno
Add 1/4 teaspoon smoked paprika, 1 cup cubed smoked scamorza, and use smoked instead of cooked ham to the pasta and sauce and mix thoroughly together before proceeding as main recipe.

### rich pasta al forno
To enrich this dish, mix 2 egg yolks into the béchamel sauce before mixing into the pasta with the ham.

### herby pasta al forno
To add a herby note, mix 3 tablespoons of finely chopped fresh flat-leaf parsley and 2 tablespoons snipped chives into the béchamel before mixing into the pasta with the ham.

variations

# tagliatelle with chicken livers

see base recipe page 115

### tagliatelle with chicken livers & sherry
Omit the chicken stock and add the same quantity of dry sherry instead.

### tagliatelle with fragrant chicken livers
Add 6 leaves of fresh sage, chopped, to the butter and chicken livers to add a deliciously fragrant flavor to this dish.

### tagliatelle with pancetta & chicken livers
For a more substantially meaty taste, add 4 tablespoons cubed pancetta to the butter and fry until crispy before adding the chicken livers.

### tagliatelle with creamy chicken livers
To make this dish really creamy, add 3 tablespoons of mascarpone to the dish when tossing the chicken livers and the pasta together.

### tagliatelle with sweet chicken livers
To add a note of rich sweetness, add a tablespoon of balsamic vinegar to the chicken livers while they are browning.

variations

# spaghetti bolognese

see base recipe page 116

### spaghetti bolognese with porcini
Add a handful of dried porcini mushrooms, soaked in hand-hot water for
30 minutes before draining and chopping. Add the mushrooms to the sauce
while the beef is browning.

### spaghetti bolognese with mascarpone
Give the sauce a creamy finish by adding 3 tablespoons mascarpone or heavy
cream to the sauce at the very end, just before combining with the pasta.

### spaghetti with chunky bolognese sauce
To give the sauce a more chunky texture, use chopped canned tomatoes instead
of passata.

### spaghetti with spicy bolognese sauce
To give the sauce some spice, sprinkle the browning beef with 1 level teaspoon
of cayenne pepper before proceeding as main recipe.

### spaghetti with sweet bolognese sauce
To add a sweet density to the sauce, add 3 canned or bottled roasted peppers,
drained and chopped, to the beef while it is browning, before proceeding as
main recipe.

variations

# ruote with pea & sausage sauce

see base recipe page 118

### ruote with pea, sausage & ricotta cheese sauce
Add 2 or 3 tablespoons ricotta cheese to the pasta and sauce when mixing
everything together to add texture and flavor.

### ruote with wine, pea & sausage sauce
Add a glass of dry white wine to the sausages and peas while they are cooking
to add a hint of wine flavor to the dish.

### ruote with green bean & sausage sauce
Omit the peas and add the same quantity of chopped green beans to the dish
to ring the changes.

### ruote with leek, pea & sausage sauce
To change this dish, use a roughly chopped leek instead of the onion.

### ruote with cannellini bean & sausage sauce
To make this dish heartier, use canned and drained cannellini beans instead of
the peas.

# macaroni with prosciutto

see base recipe page 119

### macaroni with bacon
Omit the prosciutto and use the same quantity of finely chopped good quality streaky bacon instead.

### macaroni with creamy prosciutto sauce
Make the sauce creamy by adding 4 tablespoons warmed heavy cream to the pasta when combining with the other ingredients.

### macaroni with prosciutto & taleggio
Add a more decisive cheesy note to the dish by adding 4 ounces of cubed Taleggio, rind removed to the pasta when combining with the other ingredients and mix until the cheese is melted into the hot pasta.

### macaroni with gorgonzola
For a vegetarian option, omit the prosciutto and combine the butter, herbs and pasta together with 4 ounces cubed Gorgonzola instead.

variations

# pasta with mortadella

see base recipe page 120

### pasta with mortadella & fontina
Instead of Gruyère cheese, use a different cheese such as fontina.

### pasta with mortadella & mozzarella
Substitute chopped buffalo mozzarella for the Gruyère, and use 4 tablespoons of extra-virgin olive oil instead of the butter. Then add a handful of roughly chopped cherry tomatoes together with the chopped mortadella.

### pasta with mortadella, mozzarella & lemon
To add a tangy note, omit the Gruyère and use chopped mozzarella instead, then add a teaspoon of finely grated lemon zest to the pasta when combining with the other ingredients.

### pasta with mortadella, gorgonzola & walnuts
For a saltier, more intense flavor, omit the Gruyère and use the same quantity of cubed Gorgonzola and 2 tablespoons of chopped walnuts, mixed through the pasta when combining with the other ingredients.

### pasta with mortadella & herbs
For a fresher taste, add 3 tablespoons of finely chopped flat-leaf parsley and fresh basil leaves to the pasta when combining with the other ingredients.

variations

# penne with leeks, speck & gorgonzola

see base recipe page 123

### penne with leeks, speck & gorgonzola piccante
For extra piquancy, use Gorgonzola piccante instead of Gorgonzola dolce (sweet Gorgonzola) to the leeks and speck.

### penne with leeks, ham & gorgonzola
Instead of speck, you could use cooked ham, cut into strips and added to the leeks as you would the speck.

### penne with leeks, speck & taleggio
Instead of Gorgonzola, use another soft, melting cheese such as Taleggio (rind removed) to the leeks and speck.

### penne with creamy leeks, speck & gorgonzola
To make this dish even creamier, add 4 tablespoons warmed half and half, or crème fraîche, to the pasta and leeks when combining everything together.

### penne with leeks, pancetta & gorgonzola
You can substitute the speck for cubed pancetta, fried separately in a pan until crispy before adding to the leeks.

# pasta with vegetables

Pasta combined with vegetables can be as satisfying — and is certainly as delicious — as combinations featuring mainly meat, fish, or cheese. Many of the recipes are perfect for vegetarians, meaning this collection of tasty recipes has something for everyone!

# paccheri with eggplant sauce

see variations page 164

Paccheri are a pasta shape native to the city of Naples. They are like square, flat macaroni, with a fine rib to help catch the sauce.

1 1/4 cups eggplant, cubed
1 cup vegetable oil for frying
3 tbsp. extra-virgin olive oil
1 shallot, peeled and chopped
Handful of fresh basil leaves, shredded
3 salted anchovies, washed, boned, and chopped

Salt and freshly ground black pepper
1 1/4 cups fresh tomatoes, peeled, seeded, and chopped
12 oz. paccheri
2/3 cup fresh mozzarella, cubed
5 tbsp. freshly grated Parmesan cheese

Put the cubed eggplant in a colander, sprinkle generously with salt, and place a plate and a weight on top. Put the colander in the sink or over a bowl and leave to drain for about an hour. Rinse and dry the eggplant and fry in vegetable oil until well browned. Drain and set aside, keeping warm. Pour the olive oil into a second pan with the shallot, anchovies, and half the basil, and fry very gently without allowing the shallot to brown. Add the tomatoes and season with salt and pepper. Simmer for about 20 minutes, stirring frequently and adding a little water if required. Stir in the remaining basil, and then remove from the heat.

Bring a large saucepan of salted water to the boil. Put the paccheri into the water and stir thoroughly. Replace the lid and return to the boil. Remove or adjust the lid once the water is boiling again. Cook according to the packet instructions until al dente. Drain, and add to the pan with the tomato mixture. Add the mozzarella, the fried eggplant, and half the Parmesan cheese. Mix together well, sprinkle with the remaining Parmesan cheese, and serve at once.

*Serves 4*

# pasta with zucchini

see variations page 165

This is a wonderful summer pasta dish, best prepared with freshly picked organic zucchini to really enjoy the intensely fresh flavor of this wonderful summer vegetable.

1 cup zucchini, sliced into discs
1/2 cup olive oil
Salt and freshly ground black pepper

3 1/3 cups (1 lb.) pasta of your choice
Freshly grated Parmesan cheese, to serve

Fry the zucchini gently in a very large skillet with the olive oil until browned around the edges and softened. Season to taste with salt and pepper. Remove from the heat and keep warm.

Bring a large saucepan of salted water to the boil. Put the pasta into the water and stir thoroughly. Replace the lid and return to the boil. Remove or adjust the lid once the water is boiling again. Cook according to the packet instructions until al dente. Drain, and transfer to the skillet with the zucchini and olive oil over a medium heat. Toss the pasta and zucchini together, and then tip onto a warmed platter. Serve with freshly grated Parmesan cheese offered separately.

*Serves 6*

# pasta with creamy lemon sauce

see variations page 166

This very light and simple pasta dish relies on using the most perfumed and scented lemons available. Those that have been overwintered are usually bursting with fragrance and flavor. Serve with a simple green salad, dressed in lemon and olive oil.

2 2/3 cups (14 oz.) pasta of your choice
1 heaped tbsp. unsalted butter
Grated zest of 2 large lemons
Juice of 1 lemon
1/4 cup dry white wine

3/4 cup light cream or half and half
Freshly ground black pepper
3 tbsp. fresh flat-leaf parsley, chopped
4 tbsp. freshly grated Parmesan cheese

Melt the butter gently in a large, wide skillet and add the lemon zest. Heat together gently for about 5 minutes.

When the water boils, add the pasta and cook until tender. While the pasta cooks, add the lemon juice to the butter and zest, then stir in the white wine and boil rapidly for about 2 minutes. Add the cream and black pepper, off the heat. Drain the pasta carefully, then add to the cream sauce and stir together thoroughly. Add the parsley and half the Parmesan cheese and mix again. Remove from the heat and sprinkle with the remaining Parmesan cheese before serving immediately.

*Serves 4*

# pasta with broccoli & pine kernels

see variations page 167

This is a very simple, light dish with lots of great flavors.

1 1/2 cups tiny broccoli florets
2 2/3 cups (14 oz.) pasta of your choice, such
   as pennette or macaroni
4 tbsp. chile oil

1 dried red chile pepper
1 clove garlic, peeled and crushed lightly
Handful of pine kernels
Salt

Bring a small pan of lightly salted water to the boil. Add the broccoli florets and simmer for 3–4 minutes, or until just tender. Drain and set aside.

Bring a large saucepan of salted water to the boil. Put the pasta into the water and stir thoroughly. Replace the lid and return to the boil. Remove or adjust the lid once the water is boiling again. Cook according to the packet instructions until al dente. Drain, and return to the pot.

While the pasta is cooking, heat the chile oil in a very large skillet with the chile and garlic, until the oil is just starting to smoke. Discard the chile and garlic, and then add the pine kernels and broccoli and heat through, stirring frequently. Add the cooked pasta to the skillet, toss together, and season before serving immediately.

*Serves 4*

# linguine with fava beans & tomatoes

see variations page 168

Depending upon the size of the fava beans, they may need a little bit longer to cook until tender and you may also need a little extra stock if the cooking time is extended.

2 cups unsalted chicken or vegetable stock
2 cups (10 oz.) fresh or frozen podded fava
    beans
1 tsp. Italian mustard
2 scallions, thinly sliced

Salt
1 heaped tbsp. unsalted butter
1 cup fresh cherry tomatoes, seeded and
    roughly chopped
12 oz. linguine

Bring the stock to the boil in a large, wide pan and add the fava beans. Cook gently for 6–7 minutes, or until tender, and then add the mustard, scallions, and a little salt. Stir thoroughly together, add the butter and tomatoes, and then stir again. Cook for a further minute or two, then remove from the heat.

Bring a large saucepan of salted water to the boil. Put the linguine into the water and stir thoroughly. Replace the lid and return to the boil. Remove or adjust the lid once the water is boiling again. Cook according to the packet instructions until al dente. Drain, and tip into the pan with the fava beans. Mix everything together thoroughly over a medium heat for a couple of minutes. Serve immediately.

*Serves 4*

# orecchiette with broccoli & tomato

see variations page 169

This is lovely speciality from the south of Italy, with lots of flavor and wonderful colors. Salted ricotta can be hard to find; you could substitute hard goat cheese.

3 1/2 cups (13 oz.) broccoli
2 1/3 cups (12 1/2 oz.) orecchiette
2 cloves garlic, lightly crushed
4 tbsp. extra-virgin olive oil
2 salted anchovies, rinsed, boned and chopped

2 cups fresh tomatoes, peeled, seeded and chopped
3 tbsp. salted ricotta cheese, grated
Salt and freshly ground black pepper

Divide the broccoli into small florets, removing the hard stalks. Wash and boil in lightly salted water for 5 minutes. Drain and set aside.

Bring a large saucepan of salted water to the boil. Put the orecchiette into the water and stir thoroughly. Replace the lid and return to the boil. Remove or adjust the lid once the water is boiling again. Cook according to the packet instructions until al dente.

Meanwhile, fry the oil and garlic together until the garlic is golden brown. Discard the garlic and add the anchovies. Stir and melt the anchovies, then add the tomatoes. Season and simmer for about 5 minutes over a medium heat. Drain the orecchiette. Pour over the sauce, add the broccoli and half the cheese, and mix everything together. Serve immediately, sprinkled with the remaining cheese.

*Serves 4*

# burette with almond pesto

see variations page 170

This is the wonderful pesto from the Trapani area on the west coast of Sicily, where the salt flats lie. Fabulous on pasta, almond pesto is also great on grilled chicken or baked fish. This pesto can be made in a food processor, in which case the oil should be added at the beginning.

6 garlic cloves
1 tsp. sea salt
Large handful fresh basil leaves
3/4 cup (5 oz.) blanched almonds, roughly
    chopped

4 ripe tomatoes, peeled and chopped
6 tbsp. olive oil
Freshly ground black pepper
12 oz. burette or spaghetti

In a mortar, pound the garlic, salt, and basil into a paste; add the almonds little by little and then the tomatoes. When all the ingredients are reduced to a pulp, add the oil and the pepper.

Bring a large saucepan of salted water to the boil. Put the burette or spaghetti into the water and stir thoroughly. Replace the lid and return to the boil. Remove or adjust the lid once the water is boiling again. Cook according to the packet instructions until al dente. Drain, reserving some of the cooking water.

Toss in a serving bowl together with the pesto until the latter is evenly distributed, adding some of the cooking water to help distribute the pesto through the pasta. Serve immediately.

*Serves 4*

# butternut squash ravioli

see variations page 171

This is lovely speciality from the south of Italy, with lots of flavor and wonderful colors.

3 1/2 lbs butternut squash
2 oz. hard amaretti biscuits, crushed
1/2 cup freshly grated Parmesan cheese
6 eggs lightly beaten
Large pinch freshly grated nutmeg

Zest of half a lemon, finely grated
7 oz. all-purpose flour
7 oz. semola
1 beaten egg yolk, for sealing the ravioli

Peel and cut the squash into small pieces, bake on an oiled tray in a hot oven (375°F (190°C)) until soft. Mash with a fork, and then mix in the crushed amaretti, Parmesan, one third of the beaten eggs, nutmeg, and lemon zest. Season to taste; the mixture should have a pleasant sweet/salty flavor. Allow to cool completely before using to fill the ravioli.

To make the pasta, work the flour, semola, and the remaining eggs into a soft dough and, use a pasta machine to roll out very thin sheets. (See full explanation for making fresh pasta on page 19.) Use a large cookie cutter to cut into as many discs as possible. Put a teaspoon of the filling in the center of half of the discs. Brush the edges with beaten egg yolk and top each with an unfilled disc, pressing the edges together with your fingers. Use your fingers to gently ensure that any air is removed from the parcels.

Cook the ravioli in batches in boiling salted water for 4–5 minutes or until floating on the surface. Drain and coat lightly with pesto (see recipe, page 51) to serve.

*Serves 8*

# macaroni with pumpkin

see variations page 172

Use any squash for this wonderful dish; butternut or summer squash work well too.

1 large onion, peeled and thinly sliced
4 tbsp. extra-virgin olive oil
4 fresh sage leaves
4 tbsp. dry white wine
1 cup pumpkin, skinned, seeded, and cubed

1 cup vegetable stock
2 1/3 cups (12 oz.) macaroni
Salt and freshly ground black pepper
3 tbsp. fresh flat-leaf parsley, chopped
5 tbsp. freshly grated Parmesan cheese

Fry the onion gently in a very large skillet with the sage leaves in half the oil. Add the wine and continue to cook for about two minutes or until the alcohol has evaporated, then add the pumpkin. Stir in the vegetable stock and season with salt and pepper. Simmer gently, stirring frequently, until the pumpkin is soft.

While the sauce is simmering, bring a large saucepan of salted water to the boil. Put the macaroni into the water and stir thoroughly. Replace the lid and return to the boil. Remove or adjust the lid once the water is boiling again. Cook according to the packet instructions until al dente.

Drain the pasta and add it to the pan with the pumpkin sauce. Mix together thoroughly, adding the parsley, the remaining oil, and half the cheese, and cook over a medium heat for about 5 minutes. Season and serve immediately, sprinkled with the parsley and the remainder of the cheese.

*Serves 4*

# conchiglie with creamy spinach

see variations page 173

Although you can use any shape of pasta you like for this sauce, the cup shape of this particular type holds the creamy sauce perfectly. A great sauce, with a wonderful color.

2 1/4 lb. fresh spinach leaves
8 tbsp. light or whipping cream
6 tbsp. freshly grated Parmesan cheese, plus
    extra to serve

1/4 tsp. grated nutmeg
Salt and freshly ground black pepper
2 cups (10 oz.) conchiglie
1 tbsp. butter

Wash the spinach thoroughly, then cram it into a large saucepan with just the water clinging to the leaves. Put a lid on the saucepan and place over a low heat for about 5 minutes, until all the leaves have wilted. Drain well, squeezing out any excess liquid, then put the cooked spinach in the food processor with the cream and Parmesan cheese. Process to create a smooth texture. Stir in the nutmeg, and season to taste.

Bring a large saucepan of salted water to the boil. Put the conchiglie into the water and stir thoroughly. Replace the lid and return to the boil. Remove or adjust the lid once the water is boiling again. Cook according to the packet instructions until al dente. Drain the pasta and return it to the pot. Add the butter and toss together thoroughly. Pour over the sauce and toss again. Serve immediately, spinkled with a little extra Parmesan cheese.

*Serves 4*

# pappardelle with mushroom sauce

see variations page 174

Pappardelle are one of my favorite pasta shapes — they are basically big, wide ribbons of pasta that perfectly suit rich pasta sauces like this one. Often served with game sauces, they are a traditional pasta shape of my native Tuscany.

4 large tbsp. extra-virgin olive oil
3 cloves garlic, peeled, and finely chopped
12 large fresh tomatoes, peeled, seeded, and
    coarsely chopped
2 cups (10 oz.) dried porcini mushrooms or
    similar full-flavored mushrooms, soaked in
    hand-hot water for 20 minutes, then drained

14 oz. pappardelle
2 tbsp. unsalted butter
Salt and freshly ground black pepper
Freshly grated Parmesan cheese, to serve
2 tbsp. fresh flat-leaf parsley, chopped

Heat the oil and gently fry the garlic for about 5 minutes, stirring frequently. Then add the tomatoes and stir thoroughly. Add the mushrooms and season. Stir gently and cook slowly for about 40 minutes, or until the sauce becomes creamy and the mushrooms very soft, adding a little water if necessary.

Bring a large saucepan of salted water to the boil. Put the pappardelle into the water and stir thoroughly. Replace the lid and return to the boil. Remove or adjust the lid once the water is boiling again. Cook according to the packet instructions until al dente. Drain the pasta and return it to the pot. Stir the butter through the sauce, season, and add to the pasta. Toss together, and serve immediately, sprinkled with the Parmesan cheese and parsley.

*Serves 4*

# spaghetti with grilled peppers

see variations page 175

This is a lovely, simple, colorful pasta dish, wonderfully sweet and summery.

2 large, sweet, juicy red peppers
3 cloves garlic, pureed
1 tsp. salt
About 8 tbsp. extra-virgin olive oil

4 tbsp. fresh flat-leaf parsley, chopped
Freshly ground black pepper
14 oz. spaghetti

Grill the peppers on a tray, turning frequently until the skin is wrinkled and completely blackened all over. Take the peppers out, turn off the grill, and wrap the peppers in individual sandwich bags or plastic wrap. Leave until completely cold. Heat the oven to (300°F (150°C)). Remove the peppers from the bowl and remove the skins. Cut in half and remove the seeds and membranes. Cut the peppers into strips and place in an ovenproof dish. Whisk the garlic puree with the salt, oil, parsley, and black pepper. Mix the peppers with half of the garlicky dressing, and bake while the pasta cooks.

Bring a large saucepan of salted water to the boil. Put the spaghetti into the water and stir thoroughly. Replace the lid and return to the boil. Remove or adjust the lid once the water is boiling again. Cook according to the packet instructions until al dente. Drain the pasta and return it to the pot. Pour the remaining dressing over the pasta and toss thoroughly, then pour the pasta on top of the dressed peppers and mix again. Serve immediately.

*Serves 4*

# pasta with black & green olives

see variations page 176

Because the sauce is cold, this dish is never piping hot, which makes it ideal for summer eating. Use tagliatelle if serving warm, but it's equally delicious served cold with a short pasta such as ruote (wheels).

15 black olives, stones removed
15 green olives, stones removed
2 garlic cloves, peeled
4 tbsp. olive oil
1 tbsp. soft white breadcrumbs

Salt and freshly ground black pepper
1 tsp. lemon juice
2 2/3 cups (14 oz.) dried pasta of your choice
2 tbsp. fresh flat-leaf parsley, chopped

Place the olives and the garlic into the food processor and process until smooth, pouring in the oil gradually. Add the breadcrumbs and season with salt and pepper as required. Add the lemon juice and process once more for just a few seconds.

Bring a large saucepan of salted water to the boil. Put the pasta into the water and stir thoroughly. Replace the lid and return to the boil. Remove or adjust the lid once the water is boiling again. Cook according to the packet instructions until al dente. Drain the pasta and return it to the pot. Pour over the olive sauce and toss together thoroughly. Add a little more oil if you feel it is too dry. Sprinkle with the parsley and serve at once. Alternatively, cover and place in the refrigerator for at least an hour before sprinkling with the parsley and serving.

*Serves 4*

# pasta with vegetable ragu

see variations page 177

This is a lovely rich vegetable ragu that allows you to use whatever vegetables you like best, and that are in season at the time.

1 onion, finely chopped
2 celery sticks, finely chopped
2 carrots, peeled and chopped
4 tbsp. olive oil
1/4 cup water or stock
4 garlic cloves, peeled and minced
1 tbsp. tomato puree

1 tbsp. balsamic vinegar
1 cup diced vegetables, e.g. a mix of zucchini,
    peas, green beans, peppers, and mushrooms
1/3 cup (2 oz.) raw red lentils
2 (14-oz.) cans chopped tomatoes
8 oz. spaghetti (or your favorite pasta)
2 tbsp. Parmesan cheese shavings

Tip the onion, celery, and carrots into a large saucepan with the oil and, once the vegetables are sizzling, add the water or stock. Cook gently, stirring often, until the vegetables are soft. Add the garlic, tomato puree, and balsamic vinegar, cook on a high heat for a minute more, then add the diced vegetables, lentils, and tomatoes, and bring to the boil. Reduce the heat and simmer for about 40 minutes, adding a little water or stock if necessary.

Bring a large saucepan of salted water to the boil. Put the pasta into the water and stir thoroughly. Replace the lid and return to the boil. Remove or adjust the lid once the water is boiling again. Cook according to the packet instructions until al dente. Drain the pasta and return it to the pot. Season the vegetable ragu and pour over the pasta, mixing well. Serve immediately, sprinkled with the Parmesan cheese.

*Serves 4*

# pasta with artichokes

see variations page 178

This is one of my absolute favorite pasta recipes, even if the preparation of the artichokes is a bit fiddly.

8 fresh artichokes
Juice of 1 lemon
3 cloves garlic, peeled and crushed
4 tbsp. extra-virgin olive oil
1 generous cup (8–10 fl oz.) vegetable stock

12 oz. pasta of your choice
Salt and freshly ground black pepper
6 tbsp. fresh flat-leaf parsley, chopped
Extra-virgin olive oil, to serve
Freshly grated Parmesan cheese, to serve

Wash the artichokes, remove and discard all the hard external leaves until you reach the heart, which should be pale green and tender. Remove and discard the points of the leaves and cut into four, remove and discard the hairy choke, and drop into a bowl of water and the lemon juice. In a large skillet, fry the garlic in the olive oil until just golden. Discard the garlic and add the drained artichokes, toss in the oil for a couple of minutes, then add the stock. Leave to simmer for about 30 minutes, stirring occasionally and adding more water or stock as required, until the artichokes are completely tender and falling apart.

Meanwhile, bring a large saucepan of salted water to the boil. Put the pasta into the water and stir thoroughly. Replace the lid and return to the boil. Remove or adjust the lid once the water is boiling again. Cook according to the packet instructions until al dente. Drain the pasta, reserving about 1 cup of the cooking water. Add the cooking water and the pasta to the artichokes and mix over a high heat until well combined. Season, stir in the parsley, drizzle with a little more oil and serve immediately, sprinkled with Parmesan cheese.

*Serves 4*

# vegetable lasagne

see variations page 179

This vegetarian lasagne is a great, extra-nutritious alternative to the traditional meaty style and guaranteed to be a crowd pleaser.

1 x quantity fresh pasta sheets (page 19) or
    1 lb. dried pasta sheets
1 onion, sliced
4 tbsp. extra-virgin olive oil
2 zucchini, sliced
2 medium carrots, cubed
1/2 cup shelled peas

1 quantity béchamel sauce (page 28)
2 handfuls fresh asparagus, lightly steamed
1 cup cleaned, sliced mushrooms
4 oz. tomatoes, peeled and chopped
3 handfuls fresh spinach leaves, lightly steamed
2 cups Parmesan cheese, grated
1 cup mozzarella, cubed or sliced

Preheat the oven to 400°F (200°C). Boil small batches of the pasta sheets in salted water for 1 minute (2–3 minutes for dried pasta) before removing with tongs and laying out, without overlaps, on a clean, damp cloth, or drop into a basin of cold water until required, to prevent the pieces sticking together.

Fry the sliced onion in the oil until soft. Add the zucchini, carrots, and peas. Simmer slowly, uncovered, for ten minutes or until softened. Pour a layer of béchamel sauce into a medium baking dish and cover with a layer of the pasta sheets. Cover with a layer of softened vegetables, half the steamed asparagus, a handful of raw mushrooms, 2 tablespoons of Parmesan cheese, a handful of spiach, and a handful of raw chopped tomatoes, and cover with mozzarella. Repeat until all the ingredients are used up, then add a final layer of mozzarella. Bake in the oven for 25 minutes. Remove from the oven and rest for 10 minutes before serving.

*Serves 4*

variations

# paccheri with eggplant sauce

see base recipe page 139

### paccheri with mushroom sauce
Fry 2 cups of chopped mushrooms in 1/4 of the vegetable oil, then add to the
dish in place of the eggplant cubes. Omit the rest of the vegetable oil.

### paccheri with curette sauce
Omit the eggplant cubes and instead, fry 10 ounces of cubed curettes in the oil.
Drain and keep warm, then add to the dish in place of the eggplant cubes.

### paccheri with eggplant & ricotta cheese sauce
Omit the mozzarella and replace with fresh ricotta cheese to create quite a
differently textured dish.

### paccheri with eggplant & caper sauce
Omit the anchovies and replace with 3 tablespoons drained and rinsed salted
capers, roughly chopped. Replace the basil with the same quantity of chopped
flat-leaf parsley.

### paccheri with lemony eggplant sauce
For a tangy flavor, omit the anchovy and instead add the carefully peeled skin of
half an unwaxed lemon to the oil with the shallot and basil.

variations

# pasta with zucchini

see base recipe page 140

### pasta with minty zucchini
Add a handful of freshly chopped fresh mint to the zucchini once they have
been fried until tender.

### pasta with mozzarella & zucchini
Add a finely chopped buffalo mozzarella to the pasta and zucchini when you
combine all the ingredients together.

### pasta with zucchini, pecorino & black pepper
Serve with freshly grated aged pecorino cheese and plenty of cracked black
pepper to make the dish taste a great deal more robust.

### pasta with garlicky zucchini
Fry the zucchini with 2 cloves garlic, peeled and finely chopped to give the
zucchini and the pasta a strong garlicky flavor.

### pasta with zucchini & ricotta cheese
Give this dish a lovely creamy, slightly grainy texture, by adding 2 tablespoons of
ricotta cheese to the pasta when you combine with the zucchini.

variations

# pasta with creamy lemon sauce

see base recipe page 143

### pasta with creamy lemon & basil sauce
Substitute the fresh parsley for a small handful of fresh basil leaves, torn into small pieces with your fingers.

### pasta with creamy lemon & mint sauce
Substitute the fresh parsley for a small handful of fresh mint leaves, chopped really finely.

### pasta with creamy lemon & vermouth sauce
Substitute the dry white wine for sweet white vermouth to change the flavor of this dish completely.

### pasta with creamy lemon sauce & pecorino cheese
Sprinkle the finished dish with finely grated aged and peppery pecorino cheese instead of the Parmesan cheese.

variations

# pasta with broccoli & pine kernels

see base recipe page 142

### pasta with broccoli, almonds, feta & chile
Omit the pine kernels and use lightly toasted flaked almonds instead, and
crumble 2 ounces of feta cheese over the dish just before serving.

### pasta with broccoli, toasted pine kernels, ricotta cheese & chile
Toast the pine kernels before adding to the broccoli in the pan and stir
3 tablespoons fresh ricotta cheese through the pasta and broccoli when you
toss everything together in the pan.

### pasta with cauliflower, sun-blush tomatoes & chile
Substitute the broccoli for cauliflower florets and add a small handful of
drained sun-blush tomatoes, sliced into strips and mixed into the pasta and
broccoli.

### pasta with broccoli, olives, mozzarella & chile
Add 4 tablespoons black olives, de-stoned and roughly chopped to the pan
with the pine kernels and broccoli. At the very end, when tossing everything
together, add a fresh mozzarella, cubed, for a deliciously cooling note.

### pasta with broccoli, pecorino cheese & chile
Add 3 to 4 tablespoons grated pecorino cheese and 2 tablespoons crème
fraiche to the pan when tossing all the pasta with the remaining ingredients.

variations

# linguine with fava beans & tomatoes

see base recipe page 144

### linguine with fava beans, tomatoes & mozzarella
To make the dish richer, add a fresh buffalo mozzarella to the pan while mixing the pasta and fava beans together, using extra-virgin olive oil instead of butter.

### linguine with fava beans, tomatoes & pesto
Omit the mustard, and add a tablespoon of fresh pesto to the fava beans with the scallions and salt. When adding the tomatoes, substitute the butter for extra-virgin olive oil.

### linguine with fava beans & tomatoes in a creamy sauce
To make this sauce really luxurious and creamy, add 3 tablespoons heavy cream to the fava beans and pasta in the last minute of the cooking time, and then finish off with a sprinkling of chopped, flat-leaf parsley.

### baked linguini with fava beans & tomatoes
Tip the dressed pasta with the fava beans into a buttered ovenproof dish and scatter 5 ounces finely chopped smoked scamorza and 2 tablespoons freshly grated Parmesan cheese over the top of the dish before baking in a medium oven at 350°F for about 15 minutes, or until the top is crispy and golden brown to create a lovely baked pasta dish which can be prepared in advance.

variations

# orecchiette with broccoli & tomato

see base recipe page 147

### orecchiette with spicy broccoli & tomato
To make this dish really spicy, which helps to bring out the flavor of the broccoli, add one or two dried red chile peppers to the pan with the garlic and then discard together with the garlic. Drizzle with a touch of chile oil before sprinkling with the cheese and serving.

### orecchiette with broccoli, tomato & pecorino cheese
Use freshly grated aged, peppery pecorino cheese instead of the ricotta cheese, and then finish off with a generous grinding of black pepper before sprinkling with the cheese.

### orecchiette with sardines, broccoli & tomato
For an even fishier flavor, substitute the anchovies for 2 canned, boned, drained sardines canned in olive oil. Omit all the cheese.

### orecchiette with tuna, broccoli & tomato
For a milder fishy taste, avoid the anchovies and substitute for a small can of tuna fillets in oil, drained and flaked. Omit all the cheese.

### orecchiette with cauliflower & tomato
Instead of broccoli, use cauliflower florets, and add a tablespoonful of rinsed, drained, and chopped salted capers to add an extra-sour flavor to the dish.

variations

# burette with almond pesto

see base recipe page 148

### burette with spicy almond pesto
Add some fire to this delicious pesto by including half a seeded green chile to the garlic and crush it into the salt, basil, and almonds.

### burette with almond & pecorino cheese pesto
Stir 2 tablespoons of freshly grated aged pecorino cheese into the finished pesto and use on the pasta as for the main recipe.

### burette with almond & mint pesto
Use half basil leaves and half mint leaves to give this pesto a very fresh background note.

### burette with almond & lemon pesto
Add 1 teaspoon grated unwaxed lemon zest to the finished pesto, and about 1 tablespoon fresh lemon juice to give it extra zip.

variations

# butternut squash ravioli

see base recipe page 149

### pumpkin ravioli
Use pumpkin instead of butternut squash to make the ravioli filling.

### butternut squash ravioli with Parmesan cheese
Dress the ravioli with melted butter and freshly grated Parmesan cheese instead of the walnut pesto.

### butternut squash ravioli with walnuts
Add a handful of finely chopped walnuts to the filling and dress the cooked ravioli with melted butter to change the texture and flavor.

### butternut squash ravioli with sage butter
Dress the ravioli with sage butter instead of the walnut pesto; melt 1/2 cup butter in a small heavy pan with a small handful of sage leaves over a pan of simmering water and leave to infuse for about 1 hour. Alternatively, for a nuttier flavor, melt the butter over direct heat with the sage until just browned, and then remove from the heat to infuse, and re-heat to foaming just before tipping over the cooked ravioli.

variations

# pasta with pumpkin

see base recipe page 151

### pasta with pumpkin & pancetta
Add 4 tablespoons cubed pancetta and fry them with the onion and sage before you add the butternut squash. Then proceed as main recipe.

### pasta with pumpkin & pine kernels
Add 3 tablespoons lightly toasted pine kernels to the pan with the pasta and butternut squash sauce just before you mix everything together at the end of the recipe.

### pasta with pumpkin & spinach
Add 2 handfuls of fresh spinach leaves to the pan with the pasta and butternut squash sauce just before you mix everything together at the end of the recipe, then sprinkle with 1/4 teaspoon of freshly grated nutmeg together with the last of the cheese.

### pasta with pumpkin & feta
Crumble feta cheese over the finished dish just before serving, then finally drizzle with 1 teaspoon of balsamic vinegar.

variations

# conchiglie with creamy spinach

see base recipe page 152

### conchiglie with creamy swiss chard & pine kernels
Substitute the spinach leaves with roughly shredded Swiss chard leaves for a stronger tasting sauce. In this case omit the nutmeg and add 2 tablespoons of lightly toasted pine kernels instead, sprinkled over the finished dish.

### conchiglie with spinach & ricotta cheese
Add 3 tablespoons ricotta cheese to the dish. Stir it into the pasta when combining with the sauce.

### conchiglie with creamy wild greens
Use a mixture of different leaves such as young nettles, sorrel, wild garlic, and spinach to make this sauce taste really fresh.

### conchiglie with creamy spinach & cinnamon
Substitute the nutmeg for some warming cinnamon, and use freshly grated pecorino instead of Parmesan cheese.

### conchiglie with creamy spinach & walnuts
Stir a handful of lightly toasted walnuts into the dish at the end, when combining the sauce and the pasta

variations

# pappardelle with mushroom sauce

see base recipe page 155

### pappardelle with fresh mushroom sauce
For a milder mushroom flavor, replace the dried porcini with fresh, sliced mushrooms of your choice.

### pappardelle with mushroom & passata sauce
Use canned tomatoes or passata if suitable fresh tomatoes are out of season or not available.

### pappardelle with creamy mushroom sauce
Make it creamy by adding 3 tablespoons mascarpone to the pasta and sauce when you mix it all together at the end.

### pappardelle with mushroom & mild garlic sauce
For a milder garlic flavor, leave the garlic cloves whole, lightly crushed to just crack them, and then discard after heating with the oil at the beginning of the recipe.

# spaghetti with roasted peppers

see base recipe page 156

### spaghetti with roasted peppers & anchovy puree
Add a teaspoonful of anchovy puree to the garlic puree to give the dressing extra punch — the combination of peppers and anchovies is delicious.

### spaghetti with roasted peppers & anchovy fillets
For a different way of achieving the delectable combination of peppers and anchovies, scatter about 4 tablespoons of marinated anchovy fillets through the dish while combining the pasta and peppers together with the dressing.

### spaghetti with roasted peppers & chiles
To give the dish some fire, add one fresh chile, seeded and finely chopped, to the garlic puree and then proceed as main recipe.

### spaghetti with roasted peppers & tarragon
Substitute the red peppers for yellow peppers and use 2 tablespoons finely chopped tarragon leaves, added to the parsley, to give the dish an aniseed kick.

### spaghetti with balsamic-roasted peppers
To add a sweet and sour note, drizzle the peppers with balsamic vinegar before putting them in the oven to keep warm, and finish off the dish at the end with shavings of fresh Parmesan cheese.

variations

# pasta with black & green olives

see base recipe page 157

### pasta with black & green olives, sun-dried tomatoes & capers
Add a handful of finely chopped sun-dried tomatoes and 2 tablespoons of
drained, rinsed capers to the pasta with the olive pate and mix together.

### pasta with chile & olives
Seed and chop 1 large red chile very finely, and add it to the pasta with the
olives for a fiery flavor.

### pasta with anchovies & olives
Chop 6 or 7 drained anchovies preserved in olive oil into small chunks and stir
into the pasta with the olive puree at the very end.

### pasta with olives, parmesan & pine kernels
Gently stir 5 tablespoons of Parmesan shavings and a handful of lightly toasted
pine kernels to the pasta and olive puree at the very end.

variations

# pasta with vegetable ragu

see base recipe page 159

### pasta with chickpea & vegetable ragu
Instead of red lentils, use chickpeas to add bulk and protein to this delicious sauce.

### pasta with spicy vegetable ragu
To give the ragu some heat, add 1 or 2 dried chiles to the sauce with the minced garlic, and discard once the sauce has finished simmering.

### pasta with herby vegetable ragu
For extra freshness, add a big handful of freshly chopped mixed herbs to the ragu at the every end, once it has been taken off the heat and before combining with the pasta.

### pasta with vegetable ragu & feta
Crumble 4 ounces feta cheese into the hot pasta and sauce when you mix everything together. In this instance, do not add the Parmesan cheese although you could use grated pecorino instead.

variations

# pasta with artichokes

see base recipe page 160

### pasta with artichokes & mozzarella
Add 1 cup cubed mozzarella to the pasta and artichokes at the end, when combining everything together.

### pasta with artichokes & mint
Add a handful of fresh mint, finely chopped to the artichokes as they are cooking, to add a distinctly different flavor to the dish.

### pasta with artichokes & lemon
Add 1 teaspoon of grated unwaxed lemon zest to the artichokes and pasta when you blend everything together at the end to add a zesty note to this fabulous dish.

variations

# vegetable lasagne

see base recipe page 163

### vegetable lasagne with zucchini & wild garlic
Instead of the asparagus and spinach, use lightly steamed and sliced zucchini and fresh wild garlic leaves.

### vegetable lasagne with green beans
Instead of the peas, use lightly cooked green beans, cut into small chunks and proceed as above.

### vegetable lasagne with nutmeg béchamel
Flavor the béchamel sauce (recipe on page 28) with a pinch of freshly grated nutmeg.

### hearty vegetable lasagne
For a more filling lasagne, replace the mushrooms with boiled new potatoes, thinly sliced.

### vegetable lasagne with smoked scamorza
For a subtle smoky flavor, use smoked scamorza, finely sliced, instead of the mozzarella.

# pasta with cheese

Pasta with a cheese-based sauce always makes for a deliciously comforting dish. There is a great selection of recipes here for all cheese lovers, from tangy Gorgonzola to smoky Scamorza.

# penne with ricotta & gorgonzola

see variations page 204

A wonderful combination of two very different cheeses — one fresh and mild, the other salty, strong, and complex — melted together over pasta to make a simple supper dish full of flavor and comfort.

1 1/2 cups ricotta
1/2 cup Gorgonzola dolce

3 1/3 cups (1 lb.) penne
Salt and freshly ground black pepper

Put the ricotta in the bottom of a large bowl and mash it with a fork. Add the Gorgonzola and some freshly ground black pepper and continue to blend them together.

Bring a large saucepan of salted water to the boil and use a little of the boiling water to slake the ricotta mixture until smooth. Put the penne into the water and stir thoroughly. Replace the lid and return to the boil. Remove or adjust the lid once the water is boiling again. Cook according to the packet instructions until al dente. Drain the pasta and transfer to the bowl containing the ricotta mixture.

Mix the penne and the ricotta mixture together thoroughly, adding a little more of the water in which the pasta was cooked if necessary to help distribute the cheese mixture through the pasta. Serve immediately.

*Serves 6*

# fusilli with scamorza & mushrooms

see variations page 205

Scamorza is like a drained, slightly matured mozzarella. It has a mild, slightly salty flavor and it melts beautifully into a deliciously gooey texture that winds itself all around the fusilli in this lovely dish.

1/3 cup (2 1/2 oz.) dried porcini mushrooms or
    similar full-flavored mushrooms, soaked in
    hand-hot water for 20 minutes, then drained
5 tbsp. unsalted butter
1/2 cup dry white wine

2 1/2 cups (14 oz.) fusilli
1 3/4 cups (7 oz.) scamorza, grated
Salt and freshly ground black pepper
5 tbsp. freshly grated Parmesan cheese

Chop the mushrooms coarsely, and put a pan with half the butter and the wine and cook together gently for about 10 minutes.

Bring a large saucepan of salted water to the boil. Put the fusilli into the water and stir thoroughly. Replace the lid and return to the boil. Remove or adjust the lid once the water is boiling again. Cook according to the packet instructions until al dente. Drain the pasta and return to the pot.

Add the mushrooms, the grated scamorza, half the Parmesan cheese and plenty of freshly ground black pepper and mix together thoroughly. Sprinkle with the rest of the Parmesan cheese and serve immediately.

*Serves 4*

# sicilian-style bucatini with taleggio

see variations page 206

Taleggio is a deliciously creamy, soft cheese from northern Italy, but any similar kind of cheese will also work well. Bucatini are fat, hollow spaghetti. This pasta bake is a great combination of flavors.

1 eggplant, washed and cubed
10 ripe cherry tomatoes, blanched, peeled, deseeded, and diced
12 black olives, stoned and roughly chopped
Handful of fresh basil leaves, washed and torn into shreds

4 large tbsp. of extra-virgin olive oil
2 1/2 cups (14 oz.) bucatini
Salt and freshly ground black pepper
1 tbsp. extra-virgin olive oil for greasing
3/4 cup Taleggio, cubed
Handful of fresh basil leaves, to serve.

Preheat the oven to 375°F (190°C). Put the eggplant into a sieve, and sprinkle with salt. Cover with a plate with a weight on top, and leave to drain for about 45 minutes over a bowl, then rinse and dry the cubes. Fry the eggplant, tomatoes, olives, and basil with the olive oil for about ten minutes in a wide, shallow pan.

Bring a large saucepan of salted water to the boil. Put the bucatini into the water and stir thoroughly. Replace the lid and return to the boil. Remove or adjust the lid once the water is boiling again. Cook according to the packet instructions until al dente. Drain the pasta and transfer to a large bowl, add the eggplant mixture, season, and stir together. Grease a large baking dish and arrange the dressed bucatini in the dish. Scatter with the Taleggio and place in the oven for about 10 minutes, or until all the cheese is melted. Serve immediately, garnished with a few basil leaves.

*Serves 4*

# fusilli with cheese sauce & walnuts

see variations page 207

This is a rich and creamy pasta dish enlivened with the added texture and flavor of crunchy walnuts.

1/2 tbsp. unsalted butter
1 tbsp. all-purpose flour
2 1/4 cups milk
1 cup Taleggio, cubed
1 cup fontina, cubed
4 tbsp. freshly grated Parmesan cheese

2 tbsp. shelled walnuts, chopped
1 free-range egg yolk
Salt and freshly ground black pepper
2 cups (10 oz.) fusilli
1 tbsp. fresh curly parsley, chopped

Melt the butter in a saucepan until foaming, stir in the flour until smooth, then add the milk and stir again. Simmer until thickened. Add the cheeses, walnuts, and the egg yolk and stir until well blended. Season to taste.

Bring a large saucepan of salted water to the boil. Put the bucatini into the water and stir thoroughly. Replace the lid and return to the boil. Remove or adjust the lid once the water is boiling again. Cook according to the packet instructions until al dente. Drain the pasta, reserving a little of the cooking water, and return to the pot.

Pour over the sauce and mix together thoroughly, adding a couple of spoonfuls of the reserved pasta cooking water if necessary to help slake the sauce. Sprinkle with the parsley and serve immediately.

*Serves 4*

# dischi volanti with ricotta

see variations page 208

A flat, rounded pasta shape works well with this sauce. Ruote or orecchiette make a good alternative to the flying saucers — dischi volanti — if you can't find any.

2 cups (10 oz.) dischi volanti or similar pasta
6 tbsp. extra-virgin olive oil
1 clove garlic, peeled and lightly crushed
2 tbsp. pine kernels
2 tbsp. shelled, chopped walnuts

1/2 cup fresh ricotta
6 fresh basil leaves, bruised and torn into pieces
Handful of fresh parsley, chopped finely
2 or 3 tbsp. fresh flat-leaf parsley, chopped
Salt and freshly ground black pepper

Bring a large saucepan of salted water to the boil. Put the dischi volanti into the water and stir thoroughly. Replace the lid and return to the boil. Remove or adjust the lid once the water is boiling again. Cook according to the packet instructions until al dente.

Meanwhile, pour the olive oil into a skillet and fry the crushed garlic gently with the pine kernels until the garlic is pungent and the pine kernels golden brown. Remove from the heat, discard the garlic, and add the walnuts. Return to the heat briefly to toast the walnuts lightly, then stir in the ricotta and the herbs, adding a little of the boiling water from the pasta to help blend everything together.

Drain the pasta and return to the pot. Add the ricotta mixture and toss together to distribute the sauce evenly. Season to taste. Sprinkle with the Parmesan cheese and parsley, and serve immediately.

*Serves 4*

# spaghetti alla capricciosa

see variations page 209

This pasta dish is named after the pizza of the same name, which is made with the same sort of ingredients and thus has a similar flavor, though without the egg which is so often present in a *pizza capricciosa*.

1/2 cup extra-virgin olive oil
4 cups (2 lb.) fresh, ripe tomatoes, peeled and
   very coarsely chopped
8 basil leaves, torn into shreds
1 tbsp. dried oregano

6 tbsp. freshly grated Parmesan cheese
1 lb. spaghetti
3 1/4 cups buffalo mozzarella
Salt and freshly ground black pepper
18 small, whole, fresh basil leaves, to serve

Mix the oil with the tomatoes in a bowl, add the fresh basil, dried oregano, and grated Parmesan cheese. Leave to stand for a couple of hours, or even overnight in the refrigerator.

When you are ready to serve, bring a large saucepan of salted water to the boil. Put the spaghetti into the water and stir thoroughly. Replace the lid and return to the boil. Remove or adjust the lid once the water is boiling again. Cook according to the packet instructions until al dente.

Meanwhile, cut the mozzarella into small pieces and place in a large bowl. Drain the spaghetti and add it to the mozzarella. Mix together quickly, adding the tomato sauce. Season, garnish with the basil leaves, and serve at once.

*Serves 6*

# penne with caramelized red onions & ricotta

see variations page 210

This is a lovely combination of sweet, soft red onions and fresh creamy ricotta — a real winner!

2 2/3 cups (14 oz.) penne
2 large red onions, peeled and finely sliced
4 tbsp. extra-virgin olive oil
Salt and freshly ground black pepper

5 tbsp. fresh ricotta
4 oz. smoked bacon or pancetta
3 tbsp. freshly grated Parmesan cheese
2 tbsp. fresh flat-leaf parsley, chopped

Bring a large saucepan of salted water to the boil. Put the penne into the water and stir thoroughly. Replace the lid and return to the boil. Remove or adjust the lid once the water is boiling again. Cook according to the packet instructions until al dente.

Meanwhile, fry the onions very slowly with the oil, stirring frequently, until the onions are dense, soft, and sweet. Season to taste. Grill and coarsely chop the bacon or pancetta.

Drain the penne and return to the pot. Pour over the onions, then add the ricotta and the bacon or pancetta. Mix everything together thoroughly. Sprinkle with the Parmesan cheese and parsley, and serve immediately.

*Serves 4*

# pennette with soft goat cheese

see variations page 211

This dish brings together a wonderful selection of ingredients, which taste really delicious once combined together with the pasta.

2 1/3 cups (12 oz.) pennette
5 tbsp. extra-virgin olive oil
1 clove garlic, peeled and crushed lightly
2 cups (1 lb.) fresh, ripe tomatoes, peeled and
    very coarsely chopped
15 green olives, stoned

1 tbsp. of salted capers, washed and dried,
    coarsely chopped
1 cup (8 oz.) soft, creamy goat cheese
Salt and freshly ground black pepper
Small handful of fresh basil leaves, torn into
    pieces

Bring a large saucepan of salted water to the boil. Put the pennette into the water and stir thoroughly. Replace the lid and return to the boil. Remove or adjust the lid once the water is boiling again. Cook according to the packet instructions until al dente.

Meanwhile, heat the oil and garlic together until the garlic is pungent and golden, then discard the garlic and add the tomatoes. Mix together and cook for about 5 minutes, then add the olives and capers and stir. Cook for a further 5 minutes, season, and remove from the heat. Mash the cheese with a couple of tablespoons of the boiling pasta cooking water and season with pepper.

Drain the pasta, and return to the pot. Add the tomato sauce, cheese, and basil, mix together thoroughly and serve immediately.

*Serves 4*

# macaroni with gorgonzola

see variations page 212

This sophisticated twist on a childhood favorite makes an ideal wintertime feast.

2 1/2 cups (14 oz.) macaroni
1 cup Gorgonzola dolce, cubed and rind
   removed
5 tbsp. milk

2 tbsp. heavy cream
Handful fresh curly parsley, chopped
Salt and freshly ground black pepper

Bring a large saucepan of salted water to the boil. Put the macaroni into the water and stir thoroughly. Replace the lid and return to the boil. Remove or adjust the lid once the water is boiling again. Cook according to the packet instructions until al dente.

Meanwhile, put the Gorgonzola in a large pan with the milk and cream and heat gently just to melt the cheese, stirring frequently. Remove from the heat, add the parsley, and season with a little freshly ground black pepper. Drain the pasta and add it to the pan with the sauce, mix together, and serve immediately.

*Serves 4*

# rigatoni with ricotta, parsley & basil

see variations page 213

Rigatoni are large, ridged macaroni and I think that they are perfect for this dish. This is a very quick and simple sauce that requires no cooking.

2 1/3 cups (10 oz.) rigatoni
3/4 cup ricotta
3 tbsp. finely chopped fresh flat-leaf parsley
8–10 fresh basil leaves, torn into small shreds

5 tbsp. heavy cream
5 tbsp. freshly grated Parmesan cheese
Salt and freshly ground black pepper
8–10 whole, fresh basil leaves, to serve

Using a food processor, process together the ricotta, parsley, and basil. Season, transfer to a bowl, and stir in the cream.

Bring a large saucepan of salted water to the boil. Put the rigatoni into the water and stir thoroughly. Replace the lid and return to the boil. Remove or adjust the lid once the water is boiling again. Cook according to the packet instructions until al dente.

Drain the pasta and return to the pot. Add the sauce and half the Parmesan cheese to the rigatoni and mix together. Sprinkle with the remaining Parmesan cheese and a few fresh basil leaves, and serve immediately.

*Serves 4*

# pasta with burrata & olives

see variations page 214

Burrata is the king of the mozzarella-type cheeses. It is bigger than a normal mozzarella and has a hard exterior skin (which is edible) which hides an amazingly creamy, fragrant, and delicious center. This recipe makes a warm pasta salad, perfect for summer days.

2 1/3 cups (12 oz.) orecchiette, pennette, or
  other small short pasta shape
1 1/4 cups (10 oz.) burrata
6 tbsp. rich extra-virgin olive oil
About 20 black olives, stone removed, chopped
  coarsely

Small handful of fresh basil leaves, washed,
  dried, and torn into shreds
About 20 cherry tomatoes, seeds removed,
  chopped coarsely
Salt and freshly ground black pepper

Bring a large saucepan of salted water to the boil. Put the pasta into the water and stir thoroughly. Replace the lid and return to the boil. Remove or adjust the lid once the water is boiling again. Cook according to the packet instructions until al dente. Drain the pasta and return to the pot.

Tear the burrata into pieces, drop it into the pasta, and mix well. Pour over the olive oil and mix together, then stir in the olives, basil, and tomatoes. Season, and serve immediately.

*Serves 4*

# conchiglie with mascarpone & ham

see variations page 216

This is a very delicate, simple and soothing sort of pasta dish that makes great comfort food. The conchiglie are a perfect shape, gently cupping the sauce inside them.

2 1/2 cups (14 oz.) conchiglie
2 tbsp. unsalted butter
1/2 cup mascarpone

1/2 cup ricotta
1/3 cup thick-cut cooked ham, sliced into
matchstick strips

Bring a large saucepan of salted water to the boil. Put the pasta into the water and stir thoroughly. Replace the lid and return to the boil. Remove or adjust the lid once the water is boiling again. Cook according to the packet instructions until al dente.

Meanwhile, mash together the butter, mascarpone, and ricotta. Use a little of the boiling pasta water to smooth out any lumps. Drain the pasta and return to the pot. Add the cheese mixture and the ham, and mix together thoroughly. Serve immediately.

*Serves 4*

# spaghetti with pecorino & black pepper

see variations page 215

This very easy pasta dish is a true classic and remains a favorite for many connoisseurs. The pecorino needs to be really well aged and full of flavor to add impact to the dish.

3 1/3 cups (1 lb.) spaghetti
2/3 cup pecorino cheese, finely grated

6 tbsp. extra-virgin olive oil
1 tbsp. freshly ground black pepper

Bring a large saucepan of salted water to the boil. Put the spaghetti into the water and stir thoroughly. Replace the lid and return to the boil. Remove or adjust the lid once the water is boiling again. Cook according to the packet instructions until al dente. Drain and return to the pot.

Add the grated cheese and mix together with the oil and 2 to 3 tablespoons of the water in which the pasta was cooked. Once mixed thoroughly, add the freshly ground black pepper, and serve immediately.

*Serves 6*

# maloreddus with ricotta & tomato

see variations page 217

This type of pasta looks just like small, elongated conch shells, and after cooking they always remain deliciously firm and chewy. They are a traditional pasta shape from Sardinia.

2 1/2 cups (14 oz.) maloreddus or gnocchetti
   sardi
4 tbsp. extra-virgin olive oil
1 small onion, peeled and chopped

Small handful fresh flat-leaf parsley, chopped
1 (14-oz.) can whole tomatoes
3/4 cup (6 oz.) ricotta
Salt and freshly ground black pepper

Bring a large saucepan of salted water to the boil. Put the pasta into the water and stir thoroughly. Replace the lid and return to the boil. Remove or adjust the lid once the water is boiling again. Cook according to the packet instructions until tender.

Meanwhile, gently fry the oil, onion, and parsley together in a medium skillet until the onion is soft, then add the canned tomatoes and simmer for about 10 minutes. Remove from the heat, add the ricotta and mix together thoroughly until dense and creamy, then transfer the sauce into a large bowl.

Drain the pasta and pour it into the bowl on top of the sauce. Mix thoroughly, season with freshly ground black pepper, and serve immediately.

*Serves 4*

variations

# penne with ricotta & gorgonzola

see base recipe page 181

### spaghettini with ricotta & gorgonzola

Use spaghettini instead of penne to make a dish that is quite different in texture and where the pasta will cook more quickly. Sprinkle the finished dish with chopped walnuts and finely chopped sage leaves.

### penne with ricotta, taleggio & pine kernels

For a milder flavor, use Taleggio instead of the Gorgonzola and finish the dish with a sprinkling of toasted pine kernels.

### penne with ricotta & gorgonzola piccante

To make a much stronger tasting dish, substitute the Gorgonzola dolce for Gorgonzola piccante, the much more potent and piquant version. Add a couple of tablespoons of cream to smooth the sauce if necessary.

### penne with mascarpone & gorgonzola

For an even creamier sauce, substitute the ricotta for mascarpone and add a few finely chopped chives to the finished dish for a touch of extra flavor.

### penne with goat cheese, taleggio & sun-dried tomatoes

Substitute the ricotta for creamy goat cheese and the Gorgonzola for Taleggio, then finish the dish with 3 or 4 finely chopped soft sun-dried tomatoes to give the dish a very different twist.

# fusilli with scamorza & mushrooms

see base recipe page 182

### fusilli with smoked scamorza & mushrooms

For a delicious smoky taste, use smoked scamorza and add a 1/4 teaspoon
smoked paprika to the dish together with the black pepper and the Parmesan
cheese.

### fusilli with scamorza, mushrooms & pancetta

Add another flavor and texture by frying 2 ounces cubed pancetta in a separate
pan and then stirring through the pasta with the mushrooms and the cheese
just before serving.

### fusilli with creamy mushroom sauce

Make the sauce creamy by omitting the scamorza and adding 8 ounces (1 cup)
mascarpone instead. Finish off with a sprinkling of chopped flat-leaf parsley to
give the dish extra freshness.

### baked fusilli with scamorza & mushrooms

Turn this dish into a pasta bake by turning the dressed pasta into a well oiled
baking dish, sprinkling with 2 or 3 tablespoons dried breadcrumbs, a final drizzle
of olive oil and then baking in a preheated oven at 350°F (180°C) for 15 to 20
minutes, or until the top of the dish is crisp and golden.

variations

# sicilian-style bucatini with taleggio

see base recipe page 184

### sicilian-style penne with fontina
Use penne instead of bucatini and swap the Taleggio for fontina to create a
very different kind of dish.

### sicilian-style bucatini with taleggio, green olives & roasted peppers
Use green olives instead of black and chopped roasted peppers instead of
the eggplant for a different twist.

### sicilian-style bucatini with mozzarella & pesto
For a much fresher tasting dish, substitute the Taleggio for fresh mozzarella
and add a tablespoonful of fresh pesto to the bowl when you mix the pasta
with all the other ingredients.

### sicilian-style bucatini with taleggio & salame
Add a meaty note to this dish by adding a handful of chopped salame to the
bowl when you mix the pasta with all the other ingredients.

### fusilli with ricotta
Using a different pasta shape such as fusilli, substitute the Taleggio for fresh
ricotta and in this case do not bake the dish but serve it immediately after
combining all the ingredients together.

variations

# fusilli with cheese sauce & walnuts

see base recipe page 187

### fusilli with gorgonzola sauce & sage
Substitute the Taleggio for sweet Gorgonzola to give the dish quite a different flavor. Stir 1 tablespoon very finely chopped fresh sage leaves, or 1 teaspoon dried sage to the sauce to complement the blue cheese.

### fusilli with guyère & pine kernels
Substitute the fontina for Gruyère and the walnuts for toasted pine kernels to make this dish taste different but just as delicious.

### baked fusilli with cheese sauce & walnuts
Once the pasta and cheese sauce has been combined with the walnuts, turn into a buttered ovenproof dish and bake in a preheated oven at 350°F for about 15 to 20 minutes, then sprinkle with the parsley just before serving.

### fusilli with cheese sauce, spinach & walnuts
Add 2 handfuls of baby spinach leaves, washed and dried, to the hot pasta and sauce when combining it all together to add color and flavor to this dish.

### fusilli with french cheese sauce & hazelnuts
Use camembert or brie instead of Taleggio and toasted chopped hazelnuts instead of the walnuts.

variations

# dischi volanti with ricotta

see base recipe page 188

### dischi volanti with mascarpone & scallions
Make the sauce much creamier by using mascarpone instead of ricotta and in this case, substitute the garlic for 3 chopped scallions for a milder flavor.

### dischi volanti with ricotta & nuts
Substitute the pine kernels for toasted and chopped blanched almonds and hazelnuts instead.

### dischi volanti with ricotta & green olives
Substitute the pine kernels for 3 tablespoons of chopped de-stoned green olives, which can be added to the garlic at the same stage of the recipe.

### dischi volanti with ricotta & walnuts
To give the dish a more pronounced nutty flavor, use 1 tablespoon walnut oil and 5 tablespoons extra-virgin olive oil to the dish instead of the 6 tablespoons extra-virgin olive oil in the main recipe.

### dischi volanti with ricotta & pancetta
Add extra flavor by frying 2 ounces of cubed pancetta in a separate skillet until crisp and brown, then mix into the pasta after adding the ricotta, and finish with 2 tablespoons of grated pecorino as well as the Parmesan cheese.

variations

# spaghetti alla capricciosa

see base recipe page 191

### spaghetti capricciosa with roasted peppers
To the tomatoes and herbs, add 4 chopped roasted peppers and substitute half of the grated Parmesan cheese for pecorino cheese.

### spaghetti with smoked scamorza & tomato
For a smoky flavor, substitute the buffalo mozzarella for a smoked scamorza and add a generous sprinkling of smoked paprika to the tomatoes while they are standing. In this case, omit the basil.

### lemony spaghetti capricciosa
To add a lemony note, use 5 tablespoons extra-virgin olive oil, and 5 tablespoons lemon oil, plus 1/2 teaspoon of grated unwaxed lemon zest to the tomatoes while they are standing.

### spaghetti capricciosa with anchovies, capers & olives
For a much more salty, intense and bold taste, omit the Parmesan cheese and replace with 1/2 teaspoon anchovy paste, 1 tablespoon salted capers, rinsed and dried, and 3 tablespoons black olives, de-stoned and chopped coarsely; all stirred into the tomatoes and olive oil. Leave to stand and proceed as for the main recipe.

variations

# penne with caramelized red onions & ricotta

see base recipe page 192

### penne with leeks & mascarpone
Change this recipe by using finely sliced leeks instead of red onions, and using mascarpone instead of ricotta, but proceed as for the main recipe.

### penne with caramelized red onions, ricotta & smoked salmon
Give this dish a deliciously luxurious and fishy flavor by using 6 thin slices of smoked salmon instead of the bacon or pancetta, and mix into the pasta with the ricotta as for the main recipe.

### penne with caramelized red onions, ricotta & prosciutto
Substitute the grilled bacon or pancetta with 6 thin slices prosciutto crudo, snipped into thin strips with a pair of scissors, then mix together with an extra tablespoon of extra-virgin olive oil before mixing into the hot pasta, ricotta, and red onions.

### penne with zucchini, caramelized red onions & ricotta
To add substance to the dish, add 2 very thinly sliced zucchini to the red onions and cook them together. Mix into the pasta and ricotta with the bacon or pancetta as for the main recipe.

variations

# pennette with soft goat cheese

see base recipe page 193

### pennette with soft goat cheese & pine kernels
Add 2 tablespoons toasted pine kernels to the pasta after adding the
sauce, cheese and basil, scattered over the bowl of pasta, then sprinkle with
2 tablespoons finely crumbled feta cheese or grated hard goat cheese.

### pennette with soft goat cheese & scallions
Substitute the garlic for 3 trimmed spring onions, finely chopped. Mix the
chopped spring onions with the tomatoes, olives, capers, and basil. Leave to
stand for about an hour. Boil the pasta until al dente, drain and then mix
with the goat cheese, then stir through the tomatoes and serve.

### pennette with soft goat cheese & sun-blush tomato
Use black olives instead of the green olives and add 3 tablespoons chopped
sun-blush tomatoes. Proceed as for the main recipe.

### quick pennette with soft goat cheese
Use passata instead of the fresh tomatoes to make this sauce much quicker
to cook.

variations

# macaroni with gorgonzola

see base recipe page 195

### macaroni with gorgonzola piccante & sage
For a stronger taste, use Gorgonzola piccante, crumbled into the milk and cream and stir in 5 fresh sage leaves, washed, dried, and chopped, instead of the parsley.

### macaroni with gorgonzola & hazelnuts
Scatter a handful of toasted, chopped hazelnuts and sprinkle 2 tablespoons of freshly grated Parmesan cheese over the finished pasta dish just before serving.

### baked macaroni with gorgonzola
Once everything has been mixed together, tip into a well-buttered ovenproof dish, sprinkle with freshly grated Parmesan cheese and bake in a pre-heated oven at 350°F (180°C) for about 15 minutes or until hot and bubbling.

### macaroni with gorgonzola & pine kernels
Add a small handful of pine kernels to the pasta when you add the parsley and Gorgonzola sauce to give the dish a bit of crunch.

### linguine with gorgonzola
Make this same sauce with a long pasta, such as spaghetti or linguine to ring the changes.

# rigatoni with ricotta, parsley & basil

see base recipe page 197

### rigatoni with hand-chopped herbs & ricotta
Instead of using the food processor, make a sauce that has a rougher texture by chopping the herbs coarsely with a heavy knife, then stirring them into the ricotta. If necessary, stir in a couple of tablespoons of the boiling pasta cooking water to help slacken the sauce. Then stir in the cream, season and proceed as for the main recipe.

### rigatoni with ricotta, rosemary, sage & tarragon
Add 1 tablespoon finely chopped rosemary leaves, 3 finely chopped fresh sage leaves and 1/2 a tablespoon of finely chopped fresh tarragon to the parsley and basil to really make this dish taste very herby and fresh.

### rigatoni with ricotta, parsley, basil & pine kernels
To add a bit of crunch, stir 2 tablespoons of toasted pine kernels into the pasta and sauce when you are mixing everything together.

### maloreddus with parsley & basil
To make a more delicate dish, use a smaller size pasta like maloreddus (or pennette) instead of the chunky rigatoni.

variations

# pasta with burrata & black olives

see base recipe page 198

### pasta with buffalo mozzarella & black olives
Use buffalo mozzarella instead of the burrata and proceed exactly as above, adding a little of the boiling pasta water to the dish while combining everything.

### pasta with burrata, peppers & black olives
Add 4 strips of canned red pepper, chopped into pieces the same size as the tomatoes and add them to the pasta together with the tomatoes. Finish off the dish with a scattering of Parmesan cheese shavings.

### pasta with burrata, black olives & chives
Stir in 2 tablespoons toasted pine kernels and 2 tablespoons snipped chives to the pasta when combining all the ingredients.

### pasta with burrata, green olives & capers
Use green olives instead of black olives, and add 1 tablespoon small capers preserved in vinegar together with the olives when combining together.

### spicy pasta with burrata & black olives
To add a little heat, chop a fresh red chile, seeded, very finely and add to the tomatoes, then mix everything together as above.

variations

# conchiglie with mascarpone & ham

see base recipe page 201

### baked conchiglie with mascarpone & ham
When the pasta, cheese, and ham are combined together, tip it all into a buttered ovenproof dish and sprinkle with freshly grated Parmesan cheese before baking in a preheated oven at 350°F (180°C) to bake for 15 minutes, or until bubbling hot and golden brown.

### conchiglie with mascarpone, ham & herbs
Add 2 tablespoons chopped fresh flat-leaf parsley, a small handful of fresh basil leaves, washed, dried, and torn into small shreds to the cheese mixture and season with a generous grinding of black pepper.

### conchiglie with gorgonzola, ham & sage
Add 2 tablespoons soft Gorgonzola to the mascarpone and ricotta and 3 finely chopped fresh sage leaves before combining with the pasta.

### conchiglie with gorgonzola & salame
Substitute the cooked ham with chopped salame and balance the intense meatiness of the salame with 2 tablespoons fresh, chopped, flat-leaf parsley, both mixed into the pasta with the cheese.

variations

# spaghetti with pecorino cheese & black pepper

see base recipe page 200

### spaghetti with cream, pecorino cheese & black pepper
For a creamier dish, add 2 tablespoons of cream to the cheese and oil and stir together before adding to the pasta and mixing together.

### spaghetti with pecorino cheese, paprika & black pepper
For a spicy and smoky flavor, stir 1/2 a teaspoon of smoked paprika into the cheese and oil before adding to the pasta and mixing together.

### spaghetti with pecorino cheese, parsley & black pepper
For a herby flavor and some color, scatter 2 tablespoons fresh flat-leaf parsley, chopped, into the cheese and oil before adding to the pasta and mixing together.

### spaghetti with parmesan cheese & black pepper
As an alternative to pecorino cheese, use freshly grated grana padano or Parmesan cheese, which will make the dish just as tasty but a bit less piquant.

# maloreddus with ricotta & tomato

see base recipe page 203

### maloreddus with mascarpone & tomato

For a creamier, smoother sauce, proceed as above but use passata and mascarpone instead of the canned tomatoes and ricotta.

### maloreddus with ricotta, tomato & basil

Substitute the parsley for fresh basil, ripped into small pieces, and sprinkle with 2 tablespoons toasted pine nuts at the end, after mixing everything together and seasoning.

### maloreddus with mozzarella, ricotta & tomato

Add 3 1/2 ounces of chopped fresh mozzarella together with the ricotta and mix into the hot pasta to allow it to melt slightly before mixing with the sauce.

### maloreddus with feta, olives & tomato

For a slightly salty, more robust flavor, replace the ricotta with crumbled feta cheese and mix into the pasta with a handful of de-stoned black olives

### maloreddus with ricotta & fresh tomato

Use fresh, ripe tomatoes instead of the canned variety and cook them briefly, for about 5 minutes, with the onion and parsley to retain their flavor before proceeding as above.

# pasta with fish & shellfish

The delectable fish-based pasta recipes in this chapter are all quite different; some more complicated than others, but there is something here to suit everybody.

# tagliatelle with mussels

see variations page 244

Make sure the mussels are really fresh before using them. This is a delicious and very tasty dish.

1 lb. live mussels
12 oz. tagliatelle
4 tbsp. olive oil
2 cloves garlic, finely chopped

3 tbsp. chopped fresh parsley
1 1/2 cups chopped and seeded fresh, ripe
    tomatoes,
Salt and freshly ground black pepper

Scrub and clean each mussel carefully and rinse them all thoroughly under clean, running water. Place the cleaned mussels with a little water in a wide skillet, covered, over a fairly high heat, shaking frequently to help them open up. Any mussels that have not opened after about 6 minutes should be discarded. Remove all the mussels from the open shells and set aside, carefully wiping off any trace of sand or sediment. Discard all shells.

Bring a large saucepan of salted water to the boil. Put the tagliatelle into the water and stir thoroughly. Replace the lid and return to the boil. Remove or adjust the lid once the water is boiling again. Cook according to the packet instructions until al dente.

Meanwhile, heat the oil in a large skillet with the garlic and parsley. Fry for 5 minutes, then add the tomatoes. Stir, and simmer for about 10 minutes, then stir in the shelled mussels, heat through for 2 or 3 minutes, and then remove from the heat. When the pasta is cooked, drain and return to the pot. Add the sauce and mix well. Season, and serve immediately.

*Serves 6*

# linguine with creamy shrimp sauce

see variations page 245

Linguine — long flat spaghetti — work very well in this delicately flavored dish. Perfect as a starter, or as an entree with a big bowl of salad.

1 small onion, peeled and finely chopped
1 small leek, very finely chopped
3 tbsp. unsalted butter
8 oz. raw shrimp, shelled
4 tbsp. dry white wine

Salt and freshly ground black pepper
14 oz. linguine
7 tbsp. light (or whipping) cream
2 tbsp. fresh flat-leaf parsley, chopped

Gently fry the onion and leek in the butter for a few minutes, or until soft. Add the shrimp and stir together thoroughly. Cook together for 5 minutes, or until the shrimp are nearly cooked, then add the wine and increase the heat for 2 minutes to boil off the alcohol. Season with salt and pepper and remove from the heat.

Bring a large saucepan of salted water to the boil. Put the linguine into the water and stir thoroughly. Replace the lid and return to the boil. Remove or adjust the lid once the water is boiling again. Cook according to the packet instructions until al dente. Drain the pasta and return to the pot.

Pour the cream over the shrimp mixture, stir, and return to the heat for minute or two, then pour this sauce over the pasta. Add the parsley and mix well. Serve immediately.

*Serves 4*

# bucatini with tuna

see variations page 246

This is a real favorite and a wonderful storecupboard stand by. Do make sure the tuna is canned in olive oil and is of the best possible quality for the most wonderful results. I like to make this with bucatini, but any shape of pasta will work — just use your favorite or whatever you have in the cupboard!

2 2/3 cups (14 oz.) bucatini
1 (7 oz.) can tuna in olive oil, drained
3 tbsp. fish stock or water

3 tbsp. extra-virgin olive oil
Salt and freshly ground black pepper
2 tbsp. fresh flat-leaf parsley, chopped

Bring a large saucepan of salted water to the boil. Put the bucatini into the water and stir thoroughly. Replace the lid and return to the boil. Remove or adjust the lid once the water is boiling again. Cook according to the packet instructions until al dente.

Meanwhile, process the drained tuna in the food processor with the fish stock or water, and half the olive oil, season. Drain the pasta and return to the pot. Add half the chopped parsley. and the remaining oil. Mix together, add the tuna sauce, and mix again. Sprinkle with the remaining parsley, and serve immediately.

*Serves 4*

# pasta with seafood carbonara

see variations page 247

This is the fishy version of the classic bacon and cheese version on page 37 and it's just as tasty!

2 scallions, finely chopped
3 tbsp. extra-virgin olive oil
10 oz. baby squid, cleaned and cut into small
    pieces
4 tbsp. dry white wine
3 eggs
1/2 cup freshly grated Parmesan cheese

Freshly ground black pepper
2 cups (14 oz.) penne
10 oz. firm white fish (such as cod), skinned,
    filleted, and cut into small cubes
10 oz. shelled, cooked mussels
1 tbsp. fresh flat-leaf parsley, chopped

Sauté the scallions gently in the olive oil for about 5 minutes, or until soft. Add the baby squid and cook for 2 to 3 minutes, then add the wine. Allow the alcohol to evaporate for a minute or two, and then cover with a lid and simmer gently for about 15 minutes, or until the squid is tender. Beat the eggs, Parmesan cheese, and black pepper in a separate bowl.

Bring a large saucepan of salted water to the boil. Put the penne into the water and stir thoroughly. Replace the lid and return to the boil. Remove or adjust the lid once the water is boiling again. While the pasta cooks, add the white fish and the mussels to the squid. Cook for a further 5–6 minutes. When the pasta is cooked until al dente, drain and return to the pot. Add the eggs and mix well to cook the eggs, and then add the fish mixture, season, and mix together thoroughly for a minute or two. Sprinkle with parsley before serving.

*Serves 4*

# spaghetti with squid & chile

see variations page 248

It is important to simmer the squid gently for as long as it takes to ensure it is tender. The dish will be spoiled if the squid is rubbery when combined with the spaghetti.

2 cups fresh, ripe, sweet tomatoes
3 cloves garlic, peeled and chopped
8 tbsp. extra-virgin olive oil
1 tbsp. concentrated tomato puree
4 small fresh squid, cleaned and sliced

1 cup dry white wine
1 small dried red chile, chopped finely
14 oz. spaghetti
Salt and freshly ground black pepper
3 tbsp. fresh flat-leaf parsley, chopped

Drop the tomatoes into boiling water for one minute, then peel and chop very roughly. Put the garlic and oil into a saucepan, heat together until sizzling and then add the tomatoes and the tomato puree. Stir together for a few minutes, then add the squid and seal for 1 minute, then add the wine and allow the alcohol to evaporate before lowering the heat to a very low simmer. Add the chopped chiles, cover and simmer very slowly for about an hour or until the squid is very soft.

Bring a large saucepan of salted water to the boil. Put the spaghetti into the water and stir thoroughly. Replace the lid and return to the boil. Remove or adjust the lid once the water is boiling again. Cook according to the packet instructions until al dente.

Drain the pasta and return to the pot. Add the sauce and mix together well. Season and sprinkle with the parsley before serving immediately.

*Serves 4*

# farfalle with roasted peppers & shrimp

see variations page 249

Farfalle are butterfly or bow shapes of pasta, which are available in many different sizes. When cooking them, make sure they are tender all the way to the very middle of the bow, where the pasta is doubled over to create the shape.

3 large bell peppers
10 1/2 oz. cooked shrimp, shelled
Small handful of fresh mixed herbs, chopped

5 tbsp. best quality extra-virgin olive oil
Salt and freshly ground pepper
2 cups (10 oz.) farfalle pasta

Preheat the oven to 375°F (195°C). Put the peppers into the oven to roast until blackened all over, then remove and place in a large bowl. Cover tightly with plastic wrap and leave the peppers to completely cool. Once cool, skin and seed them, and cut into small chunks.

Put the chunks of pepper into a large bowl with the shrimp, chopped herbs, and olive oil. Season with salt and pepper and mix together.

Bring a large saucepan of salted water to the boil. Put the farfalle into the water and stir thoroughly. Replace the lid and return to the boil. Remove or adjust the lid once the water is boiling again. Cook according to the packet instructions until al dente. Drain the pasta, tip it into the bowl with the peppers and shrimp and mix together. Adjust seasoning, and serve immediately.

*Serves 4*

# pasta with mussels & creamy beans

see variations page 250

Any short, smallish pasta shape will work well in this elegant dish. Pasta, mussels, and beans make a fantastic combination.

1 lb. 3 oz. fresh mussels, cleaned and scrubbed, de-bearded
Handful of fresh flat-leaf parsley, chopped
1 clove garlic, peeled and lightly crushed
4 tbsp. extra-virgin olive oil

Salt and freshly ground black pepper
2 cups (7 oz.) canned cannellini beans, drained
5 tbsp. single cream
1 1/3 cups (7 oz.) short pasta

Put the mussels into a large pan with the garlic and half of the parsley and cover tightly with a lid. Place over a medium heat and shake the pan occasionally to open up the mussels. This should take about 8 minutes. Any mussels not opened after this time should be discarded. Strain the mussels, reserving a little of the cooking liquid. Tip the mussels into a large, shallow pan (large enough to take the pasta too), add the olive oil, and season with salt and pepper. Mash the beans with the cream and some of the strained liquid from the mussels to make a thick creamy texture. Warm gently.

Bring a large saucepan of salted water to the boil. Put the pasta into the water and stir thoroughly. Replace the lid and return to the boil. Remove or adjust the lid once the water is boiling again. Cook according to the packet instructions until al dente. Drain the pasta, and tip it into the pan with the mussels. Heat briefly over a low heat, mixing the pasta and mussels together. To serve, tip the pasta evenly over the cream, and sprinkle with the remaining parsley.

*Serves 6*

# sicilian pasta with fresh sardines

see variations page 251

This dish, "*Pasta con le Sarde*," is delicious hot, but possibly even better cold the next day.

5 oz. fennel bulbs (leaves and stalks) washed
   and trimmed carefully
1 large onion, peeled and chopped
6 to 7 tbsp. olive oil
1 sachet saffron powder, diluted in 3 tbsp.
   cold water

1/4 cup pine kernels
1/3 cup (1 1/2 oz.) sultanas, soaked in warm
   water for 15 minutes, then drained
10 oz. fresh sardines, scaled, gutted, and boned
2 salted anchovies, boned and washed
14 oz. bucatini

Put the fennel in a large saucepan of cold, salted water. Bring to the boil, cover, and simmer for about 10 minutes. Remove the fennel, drain (reserving the liquid), and squeeze dry. Chop very finely. Put the onion in a large saucepan and cover generously with water. Simmer until the onion is soft, then add half the olive oil, the diluted saffron, pine kernels, and the soaked, drained sultanas. Simmer, stirring frequently, for about 10 minutes. Then stir in the chopped fennel and sardines, cover, and cook very slowly, stirring frequently. In a separate pan, cook the anchovies in the remaining olive oil, mashing them into a smooth brown puree. When the sardines are cooked through, add the anchovy puree and mix well. Keep warm until the pasta is cooked.

Bring a large saucepan of salted water, including the reserved fennel water, to the boil. Put the pasta into the water and stir thoroughly. Replace the lid and return to the boil. Remove or adjust the lid once the water is boiling again. Cook according to the packet instructions until al dente. Drain the pasta, pour over the sauce, toss thoroughly and serve at once.

*Serves 4*

# sea bass ravioli

see variations page 252

A very elegant and tasty fish ravioli recipe — the perfect dinner party dish.

4 canned anchovy fillets, soaked in milk for
   30 minutes, then rinsed and dried
1 onion, peeled and finely chopped
2 sticks celery, chopped
1 carrot, scraped and finely chopped
2 cloves garlic, peeled and chopped
3 tbsp. fresh flat-leaf parsley, chopped

3 tbsp. olive oil
4 tbsp. tomato puree
12 oz. sea bass fish fillets, poached or roasted,
   boned and flaked coarsely
1 x quantity fresh pasta (page 19)
1 x quantity tomato sauce (page 22), warmed
1–2 tbsp. mixed fresh herbs, chopped

Fry the anchovies, onion, celery, carrot, garlic, and parsley in the olive oil until soft. Add the tomato puree and simmer for about 15 minutes, adding a little water if necessary. Add the fish. Mix again and cook until the sauce is thick. Cool completely.

Roll the pasta dough out as thinly as possible. Working quickly to prevent the sheets of dough from drying out, lay one sheet of dough out on the table and dot teaspoons of the fish mixture along it in evenly spaced rows. Lay a second sheet of dough on top and press around each covered mound of filling with the sides of your hands to press out all the air. Cut around each mound with a large cookie cutter. Repeat until all filling is used.

Warm the tomato sauce in a small saucepan. Bring a large saucepan of salted water to a gentle boil. Drop in the ravioli in small batches and cook for 3 or 4 minutes each; they are ready when they float on top of the water. Drain, spoon over the hot tomato sauce, sprinkle with the chopped herbs, and serve immediately.

*Serves 4*

# bavette with monkfish

see variations page 253

This is a deliciously fishy pasta dish, best made with really fresh fish for the best results. I like using bavette (flattened spaghetti), but you can use your favorite pasta shape instead.

10 oz. monkfish tail
4 oz. sardines, scaled, gutted, and boned
1 clove garlic, peeled and chopped finely
2 tbsp. finely chopped celery
5 tbsp. olive oil
4 tbsp. cooking brandy

3 tbsp. fish stock
3 ripe tomatoes, peeled, seeded, and chopped coarsely
1 lb. bavette
Salt and freshly ground black pepper
2 tbsp. fresh flat-leaf parsley, chopped

Trim and cube the monkfish tail, discarding the cartilage. Chop the sardine fillets until reduced to a coarse mince. In a large skillet, fry the garlic and celery together in the olive oil until softened, then add all the fish. Fry together until well browned, add the brandy and burn off the alcohol, then add the fish stock and the tomatoes. Cook for about 10 minutes longer, stirring occasionally, and then remove from the heat until required.

Bring a large saucepan of salted water to the boil. Put the bavette into the water and stir thoroughly. Replace the lid and return to the boil. Remove or adjust the lid once the water is boiling again. Cook according to the packet instructions until al dente. Drain the pasta and add the sauce. Mix well, season, sprinkle with the parsley, and serve immediately.

*Serves 4*

# spaghetti with clams & tomato

see variations page 254

Quite different to the plain sauce on page 48, this is another version of "*Spaghetti alle Vongole*" and it is equally delicious. Do make sure the clams are perfectly fresh before cooking them.

5 cups fresh clams, scrubbed
4 tbsp. dry white wine
2 cloves garlic, peeled and very finely chopped
4 tbsp. extra-virgin olive oil

1 3/4 cups passata
Salt and freshly ground black pepper
3 tbsp. chopped fresh flat-leaf parsley
14 oz. spaghetti or vermicelli

Wash the clams really thoroughly in several changes of fresh water and rinse under running cold water to make sure you have removed all traces of sand or mud. Put the clean clams in a wide, fairly deep skillet with the wine. Cover the pan and place over a medium heat. When the pan is hot, shake it frequently to help turn the clams until they open up. Any clams that have not opened up after about 6 or 7 minutes must be discarded. Drain the clams and reserve their liquid. Remove and discard their shells, saving a few for decoration. In the same pan, fry the garlic in the oil for about 5 minutes, and then add the passata, strain in the reserved clam liquid, and simmer until the sauce has reduced by about one third (about 15 minutes). Add the clams and parsley, heat through, season, and remove from the heat.

Bring a large saucepan of salted water to the boil. Put the spaghetti into the water and stir thoroughly. Replace the lid and return to the boil. Remove or adjust the lid once the water is boiling again. Cook according to the packet instructions until al dente. Drain the pasta and add the sauce. Sprinkle with the parsley, and serve immediately.

*Serves 4*

# pasta with seafood ragu

see variations page 255

Spaghetti with a rich fish ragu has to be one of the most delicious of all the pasta combinations. This recipe makes quick work of this very popular dish. You could also use frozen squid and shrimp, allowing them to defrost slowly at room temperature first.

2 cloves garlic, peeled, lightly crushed but
   whole
5 tbsp. extra-virgin olive oil
8 oz. fresh squid, cleaned and washed, cut into
   small cubes
2 dried bay leaves

1 (14 oz.) can tomatoes, roughly broken up into
   large chunks
Salt and freshly ground black pepper
5 oz. fresh, raw shrimp, shelled
14 oz. spaghetti

Fry the garlic gently in the olive oil until just starting to color. Add the cubed squid and stir together. After two or three minutes, add the tomatoes, bay leaves, and seasoning. Cover, and allow to simmer for about 20 minutes, stirring occasionally, then add the shrimp and continue to cook for a further 10 minutes.

Bring a large saucepan of salted water to the boil. Put the spaghetti into the water and stir thoroughly. Replace the lid and return to the boil. Remove or adjust the lid once the water is boiling again. Cook according to the packet instructions until al dente. Drain the pasta and add the sauce. Mix together well, remove and discard the bay leaves, and serve immediately.

*Serves 4*

# smoked salmon tagliatelle

see variations page 256

A deliciously simple and festive pasta dish.

12 oz. fresh tagliatelle
1 cup heavy cream
1/4 cup (2 oz.) butter

5 oz. smoked salmon, cut into strips
Salt and freshly ground black pepper
2 tbsp. fresh flat-leaf parsley, chopped

Bring a large saucepan of salted water to the boil. Put the tagliatelle into the water and stir thoroughly. Replace the lid and return to the boil. Remove or adjust the lid once the water is boiling again. Cook according to the packet instructions until al dente.

Meanwhile, warm the cream gently with the butter and the smoked salmon. Drain the tagliatelle, and return to the pan. Add the warm cream and smoked salmon and mix together. Season, sprinkle with parsley, and serve immediately.

*Serves 4*

# squid ink spaghetti

see variations page 257

It is not always possible to buy fresh squid that have been left uncleaned, with their ink sacs intact. However, you can buy squid ink separately, in a jar; it has a deeply fishy flavor and a wonderful dark glow. Ask your fishmonger for advice.

1 1/4 lbs extremely fresh squid, uncleaned
2 cloves garlic, crushed
4 tbsp. extra-virgin olive oil
1/2 cup dry white wine

1 tbsp. concentrated tomato puree
Handful fresh flat-leaf parsley, chopped
14 oz. spaghetti
Sea salt and freshly ground black pepper

Clean the squid: Carefully separate the heads with the tentacles from the body sacs, then remove and discard all the innards, setting aside the ink sacs (be careful not to break them). Wash all the squid well under cold water, dice the heads, and chop the tentacles. Open the ink sacs carefully and drip the ink into a small bowl. Fry the garlic and oil together in a large skillet for about 5 minutes over a medium heat, without letting it brown. Add the squid, parsley, and plenty of black pepper. Cover and simmer over a very low heat for 20 minutes, adding a little water if necessary. When tender, mix the tomato puree into the white wine and add it to the pan with 1/2 cup hot water and simmer, covered for another 20 minutes.

Bring a large saucepan of salted water to the boil. Put the tagliatelle into the water and stir thoroughly. Replace the lid and return to the boil. Remove or adjust the lid once the water is boiling again. Cook according to the packet instructions until al dente. Stir the squid ink into the squid, adding as much of the ink as you wish. Drain the pasta and add it to the pan with the cooked squid. Toss everything together, sprinkle with parsley, and serve immediately.

*Serves 4*

variations

# tagliatelle with mussels

see base recipe page 219

### tagliatelle with pancetta & mussels
Add 2 tablespoons cubed pancetta to the pan with the garlic and parsley until brown and crispy, then add the tomatoes and proceed as main recipe.

### spicy tagliatelle with mussels
Substitute the parsley with a handful of fresh basil leaves, torn into shreds and half a fresh red chile, seeded and finely chopped, then proceed as main recipe.

### tagliatelle with celery & mussels
Add a stick of very finely chopped celery to the oil, garlic and parsley and cook until softened before adding the tomatoes and proceeding as above.

### tagliatelle with pesto & mussels
Add a little fresh pesto to the pasta together with the sauce before tossing everything together.

### tagliatelle with mussels, parsley & tarragon
Substitute half the fresh parsley with finely chopped tarragon to give the dish a light aniseed flavor.

variations

# linguine with creamy shrimp sauce

see base recipe page 220

### linguine with smoky shrimp sauce
After adding the wine and boiling off the alcohol, season with salt and 1/4
teaspoon of paprika to add a little spice, then continue as above.

### linguine with creamy scallop sauce
Substitute the shrimp for scallops, cut in half if they are very large and cook
them with the onion and leek for just 3 minutes, then proceed as main recipe.

### linguine with creamy & zesty shrimp sauce
Add some zest to the dish by adding the grated zest of half an unwaxed lemon
to the dish when you add the parsley.

### linguine with creamy fish sauce
Substitute the shrimp for fillets of white fish, fried gently with the onion and
leek, then roughly broken up into large flakes, then proceed as main recipe.

### linguine with golden shrimp sauce
To add a wonderful color and a touch of spice, add 1/2 teaspoon powdered
saffron to the onion and leek once softened, mix together and fry gently for one
minute, then add the shrimp and continue as above.

variations

# bucatini with tuna

see base recipe page 222

### bucatini with tuna & anchovy
For a stronger, saltier flavor, add 1 heaped teaspoon of anchovy paste to the tuna and process in the food processor together with the fish stock (or water) and half the olive oil before proceeding as main recipe.

### bucatini with spicy tuna
To make this spicy, add a roughly chopped fresh red chile pepper, seeds removed, to the food processor and process with the tuna and the fish stock (or water) and half the oil before proceeding as main recipe.

### bucatini with tuna & cherry tomatoes
Add a handful of cherry tomatoes, halved and seeds removed to the hot drained pasta with the oil and parsley, and then proceed as main recipe.

### bucatini with tuna & avocado
For a completely different taste, add one small avocado to the food processor with the tuna, process together with the stock (or water) and oil, and then proceed as main recipe.

### bucatini with lemony tuna
Add 3 or 4 teaspoons of fresh lemon juice to the food processor with the tuna, process with the stock (or water) and oil, then proceed as main recipe.

variations

# pasta with seafood carbonara

see base recipe page 223

### pasta with tuna carbonara
Substitute the baby squid for cubes of fresh tuna and the mussels for small raw shrimp and proceed as main recipe.

### pasta with seafood & pecorino cheese carbonara
Omit the Parmesan cheese and use freshly grated, hard grating Pecorino cheese instead.

### pasta with spicy seafood carbonara
Give the dish a bit of spicy kick by adding 1/2 teaspoon of cayenne pepper to the beaten eggs and Parmesan cheese and proceed as main recipe.

variations

# spaghetti with squid & chile

see base recipe page 225

### spaghetti with squid, chile & lemon zest
To add a subtle lemon flavor to the dish, add a short piece of lemon zest (be careful not to leave any pith of the skin) to the squid together with the salt and chile and leave to simmer. Discard the lemon once the squid is tender and ready to eat.

### spaghetti with squid, chile & cinnamon
Omit the chile and replace with 1/2 teaspoon fresh ground cinnamon to give the dish a much sweeter dish with a different spice note.

### spaghetti with squid & shrimp
You can omit the chile if you don't like the heat, and proceed as main recipe. Add a handful of cooked small shrimp at the end of cooking.

variations

# farfalle with peppers & shrimp

see base recipe page 226

### farfalle with peppers & scallops
Substitute the shrimp for scallops, cut in half if they are especially large, and
quickly cook them in a small pan with 1 tablespoon of olive oil for 1 minute on
each side before removing from the heat and allowing to cool before using in
place of the shrimp, as in the main recipe.

### farfalle with peppers, shrimp, lemon & arugula
Add a little bit of a zesty zing by adding the grated zest of half an unwaxed
lemon to the chopped herbs and then squeezing 2 tablespoons of lemon juice
over the peppers, shrimp, and pasta as you mix everything together, finally, add a
big handful of fresh arugula to the pasta and allow it to just wilt before serving.

### farfalle with peppers, shrimp & green olives
Add about 12 green olives, roughly chopped and with the stones removed to the
peppers, shrimp, and pasta and mix together.

### farfalle with peppers, shrimp, garlic & baby spinach leaves
Mince a large clove of garlic to a puree and mix it with the chopped herbs to add
a garlicky note to the dish when you combine all the elements then mix a large
handful of baby spinach leaves through the hot pasta until just wilted.

variations

# pasta with mussels & creamy beans

see base recipe page 229

### pasta with mussels, creamy beans & lemon
Omit the garlic and substitute with half an unwaxed lemon to add a zesty touch to the dish.

### pasta with mussels & spicy bean cream
To add bit of heat, mash the beans with 1/4 teaspoon of ground chile powder, then proceed as above.

### pasta with mussels, creamy beans & red onion
Use borlotti beans instead of the cannellini beans if you prefer, then add a very finely chopped red onion to the hot pasta when you combine all the ingredients

variations

# sicilian pasta with fresh sardines

see base recipe page 230

### sicilian pasta with fresh sardines, almonds & sultanas
Substitute the pine kernels for slivered almonds and the sultanas for currants.

### sicilian pasta with fresh sardines & tomato
Substitute the saffron for 1 tablespoon of concentrated tomato puree and proceed as above.

### sicilian pasta with fresh sardines (no fennel)
Although the fennel is absolutely crucial when making the traditional version of this dish, you could leave it out completely if you dislike the flavor, and just follow the recipe above from the point where you begin to simmer the onion.

variations

# sea bass ravioli

see base recipe page 233

### ravioli with a salmon filling
Substitute the sea bass for salmon fillets for a lovely pink filling.

### ravioli with a fish filling & lemon
Grate about 1 teaspoon of unwaxed lemon zest over the finished dish with the herbs just before serving to add a little zing.

### ravioli with a fish filling & shrimp
Stir 7 ounces very small cooked shrimp into the hot tomato sauce to add texture and flavor to this lovely dish.

### ravioli with a mild fish filling
Omit the anchovy fillets from the recipe for a milder tasting filling.

### ravioli with a spicy fish filling
Add a pinch of chile powder to the vegetables while they cook to add a little spicy fire to this dish.

variations

# bavette with monkfish

see base recipe page 235

### bavette with shrimp & monkfish
For a milder tasting sauce, use raw, deveined shrimp cut into small chunks instead of the sardines and add them to the oil, garlic and celery with the monkfish.

### bavette with monkfish & chile
To add a bit of heat, add a seeded finely chopped fresh chile to the celery and garlic, and then proceed as main recipe.

### bavette with monkfish & white wine
Use 3 tablespoons dry white wine instead of the brandy to give the dish a different twist.

### bavette with monkfish & fresh cherry tomatoes
Substitute the garlic with one small onion, peeled and finely chopped for a different tasting sauce, then add about 10 cherry tomatoes, halved and seeded to the hot pasta and mix through before serving.

variations

# spaghetti with clams & tomato

see base recipe page 236

### spaghetti with clams & chunky tomatoes
Use chopped canned tomatoes instead of the passata to give the sauce a more chunky texture.

### spaghetti with clams, mussels & tomatoes
Vary this sauce by using half the quantity of clams and half the quantities of fresh, live mussels, then proceed as main recipe, bearing in mind that if the mussels will take longer to steam open, especially if they are very big.

### spaghetti with clams & a lime-flavored tomato sauce
Add a little zing to this dish by stirring 1/4 teaspoon of finely grated lime zest and a handful of cilantro, roughly chopped, into the tomatoes when making the sauce.

### spaghetti with baby razor clams
Substitute the clams for small razor clams (or any other small bivalve) and continue with the recipe as above.

variations

# pasta with seafood ragu

see base recipe page 239

### spaghetti with a white fish ragu
Substitute the squid with fillets of firm white fish to give the dish a quite different taste and texture.

### spaghetti with squid, prawn, parsley & lemon zest
Omit the bay leaves and substitute with 3 tablespoons finely chopped fresh parsley for a fresher tasting sauce, then finish off the dish with a sprinkling of freshly grated lemon zest.

### spaghetti with squid, shrimp & anchovy ragu
Use passata instead of the canned tomato chunks for a much smoother sauce and mix 1 teaspoon of anchovy paste into the garlic at the beginning of the process to give the ragu a deliciously salty flavor.

### spaghetti with an octopus ragu
Substitute the squid for octopus, which will take a bit longer to become tender but will have a slightly stronger flavor and a denser texture.

variations

# smoked salmon tagliatelle

see base recipe page 241

### smoked salmon tagliatelle with nutmeg & fresh spinach
Add 1/4 teaspoon of freshly grated nutmeg to the warm cream before adding to the pasta with the smoked salmon, then add a big handful of fresh baby spinach leaves to the hot pasta as you mix everything together so as to allow the spinach to just wilt.

### spicy smoked salmon tagliatelle
To give this dish a little bit of a warm kick, stir 1/4 teaspoon cayenne pepper into the cream as it is warming.

### tagliatelle with gravadlax & dill
Substitute the fresh parsley for finely chopped fresh dill to give the dish a completely different taste and used gravadlax instead of smoked salmon.

### tagliatelle with smoked salmon, white pepper & sorrel
For a more elegant dish, use ground white pepper instead of freshly ground black pepper to season and add about 8 sorrel leaves, washed and finely chopped, to the hot pasta as you mix everything together.

variations

# squid ink spaghetti

see base recipe page 242

### spicy squid ink spaghetti
To add a little fire, add a couple of dried red chiles to the oil with the garlic, and discard when you discard the chiles.

### squid ink spaghetti with herbs & lemon
Use a mixture of fresh summer herbs instead of simply using parsley, and a sprinkling of lemon zest in the sauce to give the dish a fresher taste.

### squid ink spaghetti with shrimp
Stir 4 tablespoons of small cooked shrimp into the sauce before adding the ink, warm through and then proceed as main recipe.

# international pasta favorites

Pasta in some form or another is a global

phenomenon, and versions of pasta exist all over

the world. This chapter contains just a small

selection of pasta dishes from various countries and

cultures outside of Italy.

# greek tortellini salad

see variations page 273

Tortellini are available with a huge variety of fillings — although traditionally they are stuffed with chopped meat or cheese. For this recipe, choose one that will go well with zucchini and sheep cheese, such as spinach and ricotta, sun-dried tomato, or wild mushroom.

2 medium zucchini
6 tbsp. olive oil
2 small red bell peppers, diced
1 tsp. finely grated lemon zest
Juice of 1 lemon
1 tsp. fresh thyme leaves

1 tsp. chopped fresh rosemary leaves
1 tbsp. chopped fresh parsley
Salt and freshly ground black pepper
14 oz. pre-prepared tortellini
1 cup (8 oz.) crumbled feta, to garnish
Approx. 20 sliced black olives, to garnish

Wash the zucchini, quarter lengthwise, and cut into bite-size pieces. Heat 2 tablespoons of the olive oil in a skillet and sauté the diced bell peppers and zucchini for 3–4 minutes. Remove and let cool.

Mix the remaining 4 tablespoons oil with the lemon zest and juice, herbs, salt, and pepper to make a dressing. Mix with the sautéed vegetables and let stand.

Meanwhile, cook the tortellini according to the package instructions. Drain and add to the vegetables. Mix and season to taste. Serve garnished with the feta and olives. Serve warm or room temperature.

*Serves 6*

# miso with ramen & seared tuna

see variations page 274

This light Japanese broth is poured over tender ramen noodles (fine, quick-cooking wheat noodles) and topped with seared tuna to make a healthy and delicious meal.

4 1/4 cups water
4 tbsp. miso paste
9 oz. ramen noodles
4 tuna steaks (each about 4 oz.)

Salt and freshly ground black pepper
Groundnut or sunflower oil, for greasing
4 scallions, sliced

Heat the water and miso paste gently in a large saucepan, stirring until the miso has dissolved. Bring to a boil, then reduce the heat, cover, and simmer gently while preparing the remaining ingredients.

Cook the noodles according to the package instructions, drain, and divide among four bowls. Season the tuna steaks with salt and ground black pepper. Brush a nonstick skillet with oil and heat until hot. Sear the tuna for about 2 minutes on each side until cooked, but still pink in the middle. Place a tuna steak in each bowl and scatter with scallions.

Ladle the broth into the bowls and serve immediately.

*Serves 4*

# thai-style coconut noodle soup

see variations page 275

This hot, spicy coconut broth ladled over fine wheat noodles makes a delicious,
sustaining meal. Try it as a spicy alternative to traditional chicken noodle soup.

2 tbsp. sunflower oil
3 shallots, finely chopped
4 fresh green chiles, seeded and chopped
2 tsp. grated fresh ginger
2 garlic cloves, crushed
2 lemongrass stalks, chopped
4 kaffir lime leaves, shredded
1 3/4 cups coconut milk
3 1/2 cups chicken stock

2 boneless, skinless chicken breasts (approx.
    8 oz.), diced
6 baby corn, quartered lengthwise
8 oz. fine wheat noodles
1 to 2 tbsp. Thai fish sauce
Juice of about 1 lime, to taste
Bunch of scallions, sliced
Handful of fresh cilantro leaves, chopped

Heat the oil in a saucepan. Add the shallots, chiles, ginger, and garlic. Cook for 3 minutes.
Stir in the lemongrass, lime leaves, coconut milk, and stock. Boil, then reduce the heat, add
the chicken, and simmer gently for 10 minutes. Add the corn and cook for 2 to 3 minutes.
Meanwhile, cook the noodles according to the package instructions, drain, and divide among
four bowls. Add fish sauce and lime juice to taste to the soup. Stir in the scallions and half
the cilantro. Ladle the soup over the noodles and sprinkle with the remaining cilantro.

*Serves 4*

# egg noodles with sesame chicken & snow peas

see variations page 276

This is delicious warm or cold. Try taking it to work for lunch or to a picnic.

3 medium carrots, peeled and cut into thin sticks
2 1/2 cups halved snow peas
7 oz. Chinese egg noodles
Salt and freshly ground pepper
4 boneless, skinless chicken breasts (approx.
    1 lb. 4 oz.)
4 tbsp. oil

2–3 tbsp. sesame seeds
2 tsp. freshly grated gingerroot
1/2 cup vegetable stock
1/3 cup soy sauce
2 tbsp. white wine vinegar
1 tsp. sambal oelek chile paste
Pinch sugar

Blanch the carrots and snow peas in boiling, salted water for about 3 minutes, then drain, refresh in cold water, and drain well. Cook the noodles according to the package instructions, then drain, refresh in cold water, and drain well.

Season the chicken breasts with salt and pepper. Heat 2 tablespoons oil in a large skillet and fry the chicken breasts for about 5 minutes on each side. Sprinkle with sesame seeds and toss a few times to coat on all sides. When cooked, remove from the pan.

Mix the ginger with the stock, soy sauce, the remaining 2 tablespoons oil, vinegar, sambal oelek, and sugar. Mix the dressing with the noodles and vegetables in a large bowl. Slice the chicken. Serve in individual bowls with the sliced chicken on top.

*Serves 4*

# couscous with spicy fish

see variations page 277

Couscous is often thought of as a grain, but it is in fact a tiny pasta. It's often used in northern Africa as a foil to spicy dishes.

1 1/2 lb. firm white fish (such as monkfish), cut into 1 1/2-in. chunks
2 cloves garlic, crushed
3 tbsp. extra-virgin olive oil
2 tsp. ground cumin
1 tsp. sweet paprika
Pinch cayenne pepper
1 onion, thinly sliced
2 celery sticks, thinly sliced
2 cups (8 oz.) pumpkin or butternut squash, peeled, seeded, and coarsely grated
1 zucchini, coarsely grated
1 1/4 cups (8 oz.) raw couscous
1 1/4 cups boiling water
Large handful fresh cilantro leaves, chopped
4 tbsp. Greek yoghurt, to serve

Put the fish, garlic, oil, cumin, paprika, and cayenne pepper in a large bowl and toss together to combine. Place a large non-stick skillet over a medium-high heat. Add half the fish and cook, turning occasionally, for 4–5 minutes or until just cooked through. Transfer to a plate and cover with foil to keep warm. Repeat with all the remaining fish. Add the onion and celery to the hot pan, and cook, stirring, until the onion softens slightly. Add the grated pumpkin and zucchini and cook, stirring, for about 4 minutes or until tender.

Meanwhile, place the couscous in a large heatproof bowl and pour over the boiling water. Cover tightly and set aside for 5 minutes or until all the liquid is absorbed. Use a fork to fluff up and separate the grains. Add the fish, pumpkin mixture, and cilantro leaves to the couscous and gently toss together until well combined. Transfer to a warmed serving dish and top with the yogurt to serve.

*Serves 4*

# middle-eastern spaghetti

see variations page 278

This dish, with its rather unlikely combination of ingredients, is very easy to prepare and the results are really delicious.

4 tbsp. canola oil
2 small (2 lb.) chickens, quartered, skin left on
1/2 cup plain yogurt
3 sticks cinnamon
1 tbsp. ground cumin
1 tbsp. ground black pepper

6 fresh tomatoes, peeled, seeded, and pureed
2 onions, chopped
salt
14 oz. spaghetti
3 hard-boiled eggs, shelled and sliced

Heat half the oil in a large skillet and fry the chicken for about 5 minutes, turning to brown both sides. Add the yogurt; half the cinnamon, cumin, and pepper; then the tomatoes. Mix together and cook the chicken, covered, for about 15 minutes. Discard cinnamon sticks. Pour the rest of the oil into another pan and add the onion, salt, and the remaining cinnamon, cumin, and pepper. Mix together and fry gently until the onion is soft.

Bring a large saucepan of salted water to the boil. Put the tagliatelle into the water and stir thoroughly. Replace the lid and return to the boil. Remove or adjust the lid once the water is boiling again. Cook according to the packet instructions until al dente.

Drain the pasta and return to the pot. Toss with the onion mixture, and arrange in a serving dish. Put the cooked chicken on top and pour over the sauce. Decorate with the sliced eggs and serve immediately.

*Serves 4–6*

# almond & roasted pepper couscous

see variations page 279

This quick and easy dish is great as a side, or take it to work for a healthy lunch.

1 cup dried couscous
4 roasted red peppers, seeded and skinned, cut
  into cubes
12 dried apricots, roughly chopped

Handful fresh, flat-leaf parsley, chopped
6 tbsp. flaked almonds, toasted
2 tbsp. melted unsalted butter, mixed with
  harissa

Tip the couscous into a large heatproof bowl and pour over enough boiling water to cover. Cover tightly and set aside for 5 minutes or until all the liquid is absorbed. Use a fork to fluff up and separate the grains.

Toss the cooked couscous with the sliced pepper, the dried apricots and the parsley. Sprinkle the almonds over the top and drizzle with the melted butter mixed with harissa. Either serve immediately, or let cool completely.

*Serves 4*

# vegetable pastitsio

see variations page 280

This is a vegetarian version of a flavorful Greek layered casserole. Serve with a tossed salad and crusty bread.

2 cups (14 oz.) conchiglie
4 tbsp. extra-virgin olive oil
2 garlic cloves, minced
2 (14-oz.) cans whole tomatoes in liquid
2 oz. tomato paste
Salt and freshly ground black pepper
4 fresh basil leaves, roughly torn

1 tbsp. finely chopped fresh oregano
1 tbsp. finely chopped fresh thyme
1 onion, finely sliced
1 small eggplant, cut into small cubes
2 small zucchini, cut into small cubes
2 eggs, lightly beaten
1/2 cup plain yogurt

Preheat oven to 350°F (190°C). In a large saucepan of salted boiling water, cook pasta until al dente, about 8 minutes. Drain and set aside. Heat 2 tablespoons olive oil in large saucepan over medium heat. Fry garlic until golden, about 4 minutes. Add tomatoes and tomato paste, and stir well, breaking up tomatoes into smaller pieces. Season with salt and pepper and stir in basil, oregano, and thyme. Reduce heat to low and simmer for 10 minutes. In a separate pan, heat remaining oil over medium-high heat and sauté onion, eggplant, and zucchini for 5 minutes, until tender. Season with salt and pepper. In a small bowl, combine the eggs and yogurt. Spread half the tomato sauce in a medium casserole dish. Arrange the eggplant–zucchini mixture on top, then top with remaining tomato sauce. Layer pasta over tomato sauce, and spoon the yogurt–egg mixture over pasta. Bake for 45 minutes, until yogurt topping is browned and casserole is bubbly.

*Serves 4*

# malaysian shrimp laksa

see variations page 281

A tasty curry ladled over freshly cooked noodles, this is a superlative meal in a bowl.

2 shallots, chopped
3 red chiles, seeded and chopped
1 garlic clove
2 tsp. grated fresh ginger
Grated zest of 1 lime
1 tsp. ground turmeric
1 tsp. ground cilantro
2 tbsp. Thai fish sauce
2 tbsp. peanuts

2 tbsp. sunflower oil
4 1/4 cups fish or vegetable stock
8 oz. wheat noodles
Scant 1 cup coconut cream
1 tsp. brown sugar
12 oz. raw tiger shrimp, shelled and deveined
4 handfuls bean sprouts
Large handful of fresh cilantro leaves, chopped

Process the shallots, chiles, garlic, ginger, lime zest, turmeric, cilantro, fish sauce, and peanuts to a paste in a food processor. Heat the oil in a large saucepan and sauté the paste for 2 minutes. Stir in the stock. Bring to a boil, reduce the heat, and simmer for 10 minutes.

Cook the noodles according to the package instructions. Drain and divide among 4 bowls. Stir the coconut cream and sugar into the broth, add the shrimp, and simmer for about 2 minutes, until the shrimp are pink and cooked. Remove from the heat, stir in the bean sprouts and half the cilantro. Ladle the broth over the noodles, top with more cilantro leaves and serve.

*Serves 4*

# greek tortellini salad

see base recipe page 259

### greek ravioli salad
Prepare the basic recipe, using ravioli in place of the tortellini.

### greek-style penne salad
Prepare the basic recipe, using 3/4 pound penne in place of the tortellini.

### zucchini & tortellini salad
Prepare the basic recipe, omitting the crumbled feta. Instead, serve the salad topped with shavings of Parmesan cheese.

### greek tagliatelle salad
Prepare the basic recipe, using 12 ounces tagliatelle in place of the tortellini.

variations

# miso with ramen & seared tuna

see base recipe page 261

### miso broth with ramen & tofu

Prepare the basic recipe, omitting the tuna. Add 9 ounces cubed silken tofu to the broth and warm through for 1 minute, then ladle into bowls, and sprinkle with the scallions.

### miso broth with ramen & seared salmon

Prepare the basic recipe, using skinned salmon fillets in place of the tuna steaks. Sear on each side for about 4 minutes, until cooked, then finish as in the basic recipe.

### miso broth with ramen & jumbo shrimp

Prepare the basic recipe, omitting the tuna steaks. Add 12 ounces shelled, deveined raw jumbo shrimp to the broth 2 minutes before serving. Cook until pink and cooked through, then ladle over the noodles.

### miso broth with ramen & charbroiled chicken

Slice 3 skinless, boneless chicken breasts into strips. Combine 2 crushed garlic cloves, 1 tablespoon sunflower oil, and salt and pepper. Toss with the chicken and marinate for 1 hour. Prepare the basic recipe, omitting the tuna. Heat a ridged griddle pan, then cook the chicken for about 2 minutes on each side. Scatter over the cooked noodles and ladle the broth on top.

variations

# thai-style coconut noodle soup

see base recipe page 262

### thai-style coconut shrimp noodle soup
Prepare the basic recipe, omitting the chicken. Add 24 shelled, deveined raw tiger shrimp 2 minutes before the end of cooking and simmer until pink and cooked through.

### thai-style coconut tofu noodle soup
Prepare the basic recipe, omitting the chicken. Add 10 ounces deep-fried tofu cubes with the scallions.

### thai-style coconut crab noodle soup
Prepare the basic recipe, omitting the chicken. Add two (6-oz.) cans white crabmeat with the scallions.

### thai-style coconut vegetable noodle soup
Prepare the basic recipe, omitting the chicken. Add 1 seeded, sliced red bell pepper, a large handful of halved button mushrooms, and large handful broccoli florets with the corn.

### thai-style coconut fish soup
Prepare the basic recipe, omitting the chicken. Add 10 1/2 ounces cubed, skinned, firm white fish 2 to 3 minutes before the end of cooking.

variations

## egg noodles with sesame chicken & snow peas

see base recipe page 266

**egg noodle salad with sesame shrimp & snow peas**
Prepare the basic recipe, using 10 ounces raw, shelled, deveined large shrimp instead of the chicken. Fry them for 2 to 3 minutes until pink & cooked through before sprinkling them with the sesame seeds.

**egg noodle salad with sesame chicken & broccoli**
Prepare the basic recipe, using 1/2 pound fresh broccoli florets in place of the snow peas.

**egg noodle salad with sesame chicken & cauliflower**
Prepare the basic recipe, using 1/2 pound fresh cauliflower florets in place of the snow peas.

**egg noodle salad with sesame chicken, snow peas & scallions**
Prepare the basic recipe, sprinkling the salad with 5 sliced scallions before dressing.

**egg noodle salad with sesame chicken & green peppers**
Prepare the basic recipe, omitting the snow peas. Instead, add 2 sliced, seeded green peppers to the noodles & carrots before dressing.

# couscous with spicy fish

see base recipe page 266

### couscous with spicy chicken
Use chicken fillets, cut into 1 1/2-inch chunks and proceed as main recipe, making sure the chicken in thoroughly cooked.

### couscous with spicy tofu
To make this a vegetarian dish, substitute the fish for firm tofu, cut into small chunks, and proceed as main recipe, taking care not to break up the tofu.

### couscous with spicy jumbo shrimp
Use jumbo shrimp, heads, tails, and shells removed, and cut into 3 pieces each, instead of the fish, to make this dish more luxurious.

### colorful couscous with spicy fish
Add color and sweetness to the dish by adding 2 coarsely grated medium sized carrots to the onion and celery.

### couscous with curried fish
To change the flavor completely, use 6 teaspoon mild curry powder instead of the cumin, paprika and cayenne pepper, and proceed as main recipe.

variations

# middle-eastern spaghetti

see base recipe page 267

### spicy middle eastern spaghetti
Prepare the basic recipe, adding 2 whole dried red chile peppers to the onion and spice mixture. Discard the chiles with the cinnamon sticks.

### middle eastern spaghetti with fish
Prepare the basic recipe, replacing the chicken with thick, skinless fish fillets. Reduce the cooking time by about half so that the fish does not overcook.

### middle eastern spaghetti with lamb
Prepare the basic recipe, replacing the chicken with 8–12 small lamb chops or cutlets.

variations

# almond & roasted pepper couscous

see base recipe page 268

### sweet couscous with almonds & roasted pepper
Substitute the dried apricots for chopped stoned prunes to give the couscous a sweeter flavor.

### almond & spicy roasted pepper couscous
Add 2 mild chiles, seeded and coarsely chopped when roasting the peppers.

### walnut & roasted pepper couscous
Substitute the almonds for lightly toasted chopped walnuts to vary the flavor.

### almond & green bean couscous
Substitute the peppers for 1 1/2 cups green beans, cooked and chopped, to change the flavor and color of the dish.

### almond, sweet corn & roasted pepper couscous
Add 6 tablespoon canned sweet corn to add color and flavor to the dish.

variations

# vegetable pastitsio

see base recipe page 271

### pastitsio with ground lamb
Prepare the basic recipe, adding 1 pound ground lamb to the tomato sauce.
Brown lamb with the garlic. Drain and proceed with recipe.

### pastitsio with ground beef
Prepare the basic recipe, adding 1 pound ground beef to the tomato sauce.
Brown beef with the garlic. Drain and proceed with recipe.

### pastitsio with macaroni
Prepare the basic recipe, replacing the shell-shaped pasta with an equal
quantity of macaroni.

### pastitsio with béchamel
Prepare the basic recipe, replacing the yogurt–egg topping with 1/2 quantity
béchamel sauce recipe (page 28). Spoon over pasta and bake as directed.

### spicy vegetable pastitsio
Prepare the basic recipe, adding 2 chopped fresh chiles (or to taste) to the
tomato sauce with the garlic.

variations

# malaysian shrimp laksa

see base recipe page 272

### malaysian salmon laksa
Prepare the basic recipe, using 3 skinned, cubed 5-ounce salmon fillets in place of the shrimp.

### malaysian shrimp laksa with rice noodles
Prepare the basic recipe, using flat rice noodles in place of wheat noodles.

### malaysian shrimp laksa with scallions
Prepare the basic recipe, adding 1 bunch of sliced scallions with the bean sprouts.

### vegetarian laksa
Prepare the basic recipe omitting the fish sauce and shrimp, and seasoning with salt. Add 10 ounces cubed tofu and warm through for 1 minute before adding the bean sprouts and cilantro.

### malaysian chicken laksa
Prepare the basic recipe, adding 2 skinless, boneless chicken breasts, sliced into small bite-size pieces, with the stock and coconut milk.

# index

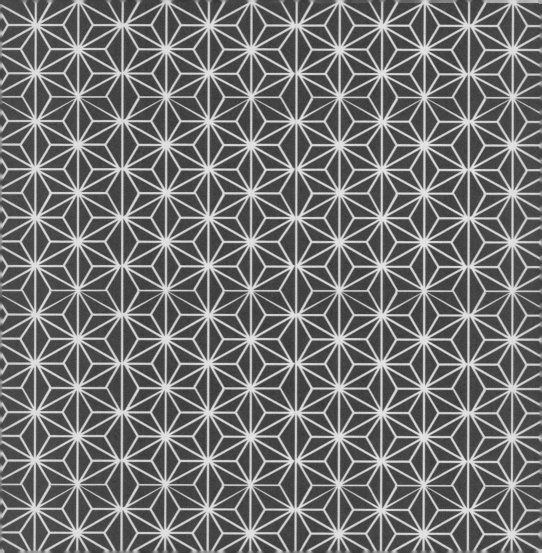